Why Smart Kids Worry

And What Parents Can Do to Help

ALLISON EDWARDS, LPC

sourcebooks

Photo one, page 7, courtesy of www.photos-public-domain.com.
Photo two, page 7, courtesy of www.aaps.k12.mi.us.
Photo three, page 99, courtesy of Allison Edwards.

This publication is designed to provide accurate and authoritative information in regard to the subject matter covered. It is sold with the understanding that the publisher is not engaged in rendering legal, accounting, or other professional service. If legal advice or other expert assistance is required, the services of a competent professional person should be sought. —*From a Declaration of Principles Jointly Adopted by a Committee of the American Bar Association and a Committee of Publishers and Associations*

This book is not intended as a substitute for medical advice from a qualified physician. The intent of this book is to provide accurate general information in regard to the subject matter covered. If medical advice or other expert help is needed, the services of an appropriate medical professional should be sought.

Published by Sourcebooks, Inc.
P.O. Box 4410, Naperville, Illinois 60567-4410
(630) 961-3900
Fax: (630) 961-2168
www.sourcebooks.com

Edwards, Allison.
  Why smart kids worry : and what parents can do to help / Allison Edwards.
     pages cm
  Includes index.
  (pbk. : alk. paper) 1. Anxiety in children. 2. Adjustment (Psychology) in children. 3. Parenting. I. Title.
  BF723.A5.E393 2013
  155.4'1246—dc23

                          2013017033

Printed and bound in the United States of America.
VP 10 9 8 7 6 5 4 3 2 1

Contents

• •

Introduction

· ·

Five-year-old Thomas is worried about death. He is afraid his parents are going to die, along with his grandparents, his dog, and his best friend. "Mommy, I'm scared," Thomas says each night before bedtime. "What if you and Daddy die while I'm sleeping?" Although Thomas is in kindergarten, he's reading on a fourth-grade level. He is well liked, has lots of friends, and comes from a stable home. "I don't know why this is happening," his mother says. "He doesn't know anyone who has died. I don't allow him to watch scary movies. He's only five. How can he already be worrying about death?"

After receiving a B on her last math test, eight-year-old Cassandra worries she won't get into college. "I used to get all A's and now that I'm getting B's, I'll never get into college." Cassandra's mother is dumbfounded by her daughter's remarks. "We don't talk about college at home. I don't expect A's. I don't understand why she's worried about something ten years from now."

Eleven-year-old Madeline worries her parents are getting a divorce. "I heard my parents fighting last night and I'm scared they're getting a divorce. Sarah's parents got divorced last year and now she only gets to see her dad on the weekends." Madeline's mother and father have no intention of getting a divorce and are frustrated by Madeline's reaction to their small argument. "Madeline's always taking things to the next level," her mother says. "I can't get her to understand that sometimes parents fight. It doesn't mean we are getting a divorce. I don't know what to do."

Anxiety is the number-one mental-health issue among children in the United States, and it has held that spot for over a decade. It also happens to be the number-one mental-health issue among adults in the United States, so it's apparent the apple doesn't fall far from the tree.

We're an extremely anxious nation.

What happens between childhood and adulthood? Are the anxious adults of today the product of the anxious kids of the '50s, '60s, and '70s? Will the anxious kids of today become the anxious adults of the future? Research tells us the human brain is most malleable in childhood, and as we grow older, our brains become less likely to change. What is relatively simple to change for a five-year-old is difficult to change for a fifty-five-year-old.

As a psychotherapist, I see this time and time again. I might see a severely anxious seven-year-old, and after giving the parents some tools and working with the child for a short period of time, the child improves remarkably. Then I see a severely anxious middle-aged adult, and the situation looks very different. Things move much slower. They are much harder to change. That's because the negative patterns have existed longer, and they've seeped into the cracks of everyday life. Quite often, issues that could have been remedied in a person's childhood become large obstacles in his or her adulthood.

The best time to help an anxious person is during childhood. Before patterns become too ingrained and self-esteem is too low, kids (and their parents) need the resources to turn things around.

This is what this book is intended to do: give parents the information and tools they need to help their children with anxiety. Specifically, to give the parents of smart kids what they need to help their children. As you will see in this book, smart kids think differently than regular kids, and you must parent them differently. We'll get into the definition of smart later, but for now it's important to know that smart kids worry about different things than regular kids, so you must be prepared to handle the fears they bring to the table.

I suspect you have a child who is smart, talented beyond his years, yet troubled by advanced-level fears he or she is unequipped to handle. Your child has likely asked you questions you don't know how to answer, and your child may seem more advanced than you remember being at the same age. He is processing new information so quickly you can't seem to keep up.

While a vast number of smart kids struggle with anxiety, there have been very few books that directly address this issue. There are a variety of books about raising smart children, as well as books about how to parent anxious children, but virtually no information on how to raise a smart *and* anxious child. This book fills the gap. With the case studies, practical information, and parenting tools included in this book, you will be able to help your bright, precocious child be happier and more equipped to handle his anxiety.

Most books out there focus on how to "fix" your child's anxiety rather than on how to connect with your child during anxious moments. This book is different. The information and tools included in this book are not intended to make your child's anxiety go away; rather, they are intended to help your child channel his anxiety. In a "fix it" world, we are often searching for the next thing that will make it all better. When we try to "fix" kids, we send the message that they aren't good enough. When we help them accept the part of them that worries and help them channel their anxiety, we empower them. It takes only a brief look at the retail and diet industries to realize that quick fixes don't last. Quick fixes often put us at a worse place than where we started.

That being said, your child's anxiety can greatly improve if you commit to becoming the kind of parent your child needs during anxious moments. That does not mean rescuing your child or solving problems for him; it simply means understanding the way your child thinks and applying the right tools to help him be more independent. Your child will ultimately need to be able to process fears on his own, and when you provide a safe, nurturing environment while setting appropriate boundaries, you allow him to do just that.

How to Use This Book

This book is divided into two parts. Part One is designed to give you the information you need to parent your anxious child. It explains the minds of smart kids and the effects of anxiety on children. Part One will also help you determine what kind of anxiety your child has, along with how he or she processes it. Most importantly, Part One will help you determine what tools will be most effective for your child. It is very important to read Part One in its entirety so you will have the information you need to successfully implement the tools in Part Two.

Part Two contains fifteen tools to help you parent your anxious child. The beginning of Part Two explains how to go through each tool, but it is important to keep in mind from the outset that more is less when it comes to using the tools. Instead of going through the section saying, "Oh, that'll work! That'll work too. I'll try that!" take some time to think about what will truly work best for your child. There is no rush in implementing the tools. It's more important to understand and be patient when selecting the tool that will work best with your child.

A Final Note

I have had the privilege to work with hundreds of anxious kids over the past ten years. Each child helped me learn, not only professionally, but also personally, and I value each child I've had the joy of working with. The case studies I use in this book are real cases; however, the identities of the children have been protected. I changed the names and genders of the children but kept the ages consistent to make the developmental stages applicable. I also use "he" when referring to both genders as a way to keep the language simple and consistent.

This book will help you understand your child in a new way. It will also give you tools to transform your parenting and, as a result, transform the way your child deals with anxiety. Ultimately, I hope that from reading this book, you develop a deeper connection with your child. Regardless of what your child faces in the upcoming years, you will have the knowledge and tools to help him navigate whatever comes his way.

Part One

How Smart Kids Think

This section helps you understand what your child is going through. As you read through the information, I would encourage you to be open to thinking about your child differently. Part One was written through the eyes of a child, not of an adult, so there may be some new information about anxiety and intelligence you have not heard before. Take in the information, let it soak in, and see how it applies to your child. The information in Part One is taken from countless hours spent with anxious kids and what they have described experiencing. I use phrases like "a gerbil on a wheel" and "emotional tank" as examples of the language kids have used to describe what their inner worlds feel like.

Part One also includes concrete examples of how to talk to kids about their anxiety. In this section, I encourage you to use the word "worry" instead of "anxiety" and to use other kid-friendly language. This takes anxiety down to the level of the child, instead of raising it to the level of the adult. The language you use with anxious kids is very important: it is one of the ways parents can help kids become more aware of themselves and ultimately manage their own anxiety.

Finally, it's important to read Part One thoroughly before jumping to the tools. While the tools are important, the information in this section is even more important. To know what will work best for your child, you must first understand how your child thinks, how he processes anxiety, and what role you need to play as a parent.

1

The New Definition of "Smart"

· ·

When you say the word "smart," do you think of a doctor, lawyer, or the valedictorian of your high school class? The words *summa cum laude* and "36 on the ACT" may come to mind, as well as prestigious universities such as Harvard, Yale, and Princeton. But what many people don't realize is that a college dropout may be smarter than a Rhodes scholar. A high-school dropout may be smarter than a college graduate, and the plumber who fixes the CEO's toilet may be smarter than the CEO. Traditionally, when we think of "intelligence," we are actually thinking of achievement, swapping one for the other instead of seeing them as distinctly different.

Twenty years ago, if you were smart, you went to college and became a business person, attorney, or doctor and made more money than most people around you. Now that we're in the information age, some of the smartest people are bypassing college altogether to start their own businesses or internet companies, or even travel the world. The new definition of intelligence is to think outside the box and create something no one has seen before. It can be as simple as a gadget, website, or a device to hold your laptop, but the world no longer measures the smartest people by degrees and grade-point averages.

Many parents believe their child is smart but aren't sure how he measures up to other kids. If he is certified gifted or does really well in school, they have concrete evidence of their child's abilities. If not, they aren't sure if their child is that much different from everyone else. When parents walk in my office and say, "My child is smart. He doesn't do that well at school, but he seems more advanced than other kids," I help parents redefine what being smart can look like.

Smart Kid = the ability to take ideas/skills to the next level

By taking an idea to the next level, I mean the ability to take a thought, idea, skill, or concept to a level in which it was not presented. Here are some examples of how smart kids think versus the average kid:

Average Kid	Smart Kid
$8 + 2 = 10$	$8 + 2 = 5 + 5$
I see a snake.	I see a boa constrictor.
I'm 10 years old.	I've lived ⅛ of my life..
I'm different.	I'm an anomaly.
Some people die.	I may be one of them.
Pollution is bad.	It's destroying the Earth.
My parents are fighting.	They're getting a divorce.
I feel scared.	I may never feel safe again.

While taking concepts to the next level can be a great asset for kids, it can also be a problem. The ability to take ideas to the next level opens a world for smart kids that they are ill-equipped to handle. What's more, the problem is actually getting worse. As a culture, we are becoming smarter every year, and as intelligence rises, so does the amount of higher-level thinking smart kids are capable of.

The Flynn Effect

Are today's kids smarter than we were?

According to James R. Flynn, founder of the "Flynn Effect," average intelligence jumps 3 points per decade among children in the United States. Regardless of schooling, exposure to academic activities, tutoring, or Baby Einstein, Flynn found that IQ rises. The number of people who score high enough to be classified as "genius" has increased more than twenty times over the last generation. Flynn describes this as "a cultural renaissance too great to be overlooked." Whether people are displaying increased overall intelligence or simply advanced problem-solving abilities, the number of scientific and technological discoveries made by great minds suggests we are in a time like no other.

So what does this mean? It means today's kids are outsmarting their parents. They win almost every argument, find information on the Internet you didn't even know existed, and remember everything you said that you wished you hadn't. I continually hear, "I just can't keep up with him. He seems so advanced. I don't remember trying to pull those things when I was his age. Something must be wrong." The truth is, kids are pulling things today we didn't pull as kids because today's kids are smarter.

The Seven Types of Intelligence

When you look at intelligence, it's important to see the big picture. Psychologists and researchers have been debating the definition of intelligence for over fifty years, and in 1983, a man by the name of Howard Gardner put his ideas into a theory he called multiple intelligences. Gardner believed there are different types of intelligence, and that simply measuring kids by how they perform in school is not an accurate measure of how smart they really are. For example, a child who learns how to multiply easily is not necessarily smarter than a child who doesn't. The child who is slower to learn may be smarter than the child who is quicker. What looks like slowness may be hiding a mathematical intelligence potentially higher than that of a child who just memorizes the multiplication tables. Gardner broke his theory down into seven categories, which he called **The Seven Types of Intelligence**.

1. **Linguistic**—the capacity to use language effectively as a means of expression and communication through the written or spoken word (example: Shakespeare)
2. **Logical-Mathematical**—the ability to recognize relationships and patterns between concepts and things, to think logically, to calculate numbers, and to solve problems scientifically and systematically (example: Einstein)
3. **Visual-Spatial**—the ability to think in images and orient oneself spatially (example: Picasso)
4. **Musical**—the capacity to use music as a vehicle of expression. Musically intelligent people are perceptive to elements of rhythm, melody, and pitch (example: Mozart)
5. **Bodily-Kinesthetic**—the capacity of using one's own body skillfully as a means of expression or to work with one's body to create or manipulate objects (example: Michael Jordan)

6. **Interpersonal**—the capacity to appropriately and effectively communicate with and respond to other people (example: Oprah)
7. **Intrapersonal**—the capacity to accurately know one's self, including knowledge of one's own strengths, motivations, goals, and feelings (example: Freud)

Example #1: A second-grade art teacher asks the class to draw a tree.

A child with average Visual-Spatial Intelligence will draw a tree like this:

A child with advanced Visual-Spatial Intelligence will draw a tree like this:

Example #2: Parents get in an argument over money in front of their two children.

A child with average Interpersonal Intelligence will think:

My parents are fighting about money again.

A child with advanced Interpersonal Intelligence will notice that his parents' body language has changed since the last argument and think:

My parents are going to get a divorce over money. I really shouldn't ask for anything for my birthday this year. Maybe they'll stay together if I don't, because then they'll have more money.

In both examples, two children were exposed to the same stimuli, but each reacted to it very differently.

Example #3: A parent picks up her son early from school because he's sick.

A child with average Interpersonal Intelligence will think:

Mom picked Henry up from school because he's sick.

A child with advanced Interpersonal Intelligence will think:

Mom picked Henry up from school because she loves him more. She picked him up last week too. I really don't think Henry's sick. I think Mom just wants to spend more time with him. I wish Mom would love me as much as she loves Henry.

These are all examples of smart kids who may or may not be successful at school. The child in Example #1 is a superior artist but may have a processing disorder. She may spend her time drawing instead of doing her work and may get into trouble for being distracted by her art, because that's all she really wants to do. Chances are the classroom teacher won't see the child in Example #1 as smart. Chances are the art teacher will, though. He might even see her as gifted. So who's right? The classroom teacher or the art teacher? It all depends on what they specialize in. The classroom teacher specializes in Logical-Mathematical Intelligence, and the art teacher specializes in Visual-Spatial Intelligence.

The children in Example #2 and Example #3 are what many therapists are seeing in their offices. Kids with high Interpersonal Intelligence are the kids who are highly sensitive, highly perceptive, and who take relational experiences to the next level. They pick up on the slightest changes within the family system and react to them with high amounts of emotion. They are always tuned into how much attention little brother is getting and to how their friends are perceiving them. This high attunement means they may have a hard time shutting off what's going on around them.

You may look at the Seven Types of Intelligence and know exactly where your child fits, or you may be unsure. Your child might be great athlete and therefore have a high level of Bodily-Kinesthetic Intelligence. He may also be a great listener and friend, and therefore have a high level of Interpersonal Intelligence. He may also struggle in art class, and therefore have a lower Visual-Spatial Intelligence. This does not mean your child is going to grow up to be a likable, professional athlete. It just means that right now, these are the areas he finds success in. In other words, these are the areas where he has natural abilities.

Natural Abilities vs. Hard Work

Just because your child is smart doesn't mean he's going to succeed at everything. Even if he puts in the extra effort, he still may not be as successful as some of his peers.

When I was ten years old, I decided I wanted to be a college basketball player. That summer I asked my dad for a basketball hoop, a weight set, and a jump rope. By the next year, I was the best basketball player in my grade. At eleven, I thought if I worked hard enough, I could play at the University of Connecticut, a premier powerhouse, and maybe even become a professional basketball player. But what I learned throughout middle and high school is that you can't practice quickness. You can't practice jumping abilities, and you can't make yourself taller. By my senior year I was a five-foot, seven-inch shooting guard who managed to get a basketball scholarship…but not to UConn.

That spring, I read an article about a girl who'd just started playing basketball her junior year. She was six-foot-three, could touch the rim, and was going to a top-ranked Division I school. I remember feeling defeated and overwhelmed by the sheer number of hours I had spent training that she hadn't.

But what I realize now is that the hard work did pay off—just not in basketball. The discipline it took to stick to my training routine has shaped the rest of my life. During my senior year in high school, however, I couldn't see that.

That natural abilities sometimes override hard work is a difficult dynamic for kids to understand. Some kids spend hours doing homework, while other kids finish in fifteen minutes. Some kids kick a goal in their first soccer game, while other kids don't make one all season. When kids put effort into succeeding and they don't measure up to their peers, their reality shifts. Common sense says, *If I work hard, I'll succeed*, but that's not always the case.

The Expectation of Success

How does this make kids anxious? Many smart kids expect to be good at one thing just because they're good at another. They don't need to practice in the activity that fits their natural ability, so why should they practice at another sport, skill, or class? Kids who excel in Logical-Mathematical Intelligence may expect to be the best player on the soccer team, and Bodily-Kinesthetic kids who earn the highest belt in karate class expect to receive the greatest applause at the piano recital. If these expectations aren't met, they'll often become frustrated and either make excuses or want to quit.

If this sounds like your child, it's important to remind him that effort is just as important as success. Reward your child for spending two hours practicing kicking goals rather than scoring two goals in a game. After your child practices for an hour, take him out for ice cream. After he practices for a month, buy him a new soccer ball or a new soccer shirt.

It's also important to show empathy for your child's frustration (more about empathy later). Many smart kids have never experienced failure, and by acknowledging this, you let them know you understand what they're going through. You can recognize your child's sadness or frustration by saying, "I know you don't want to go to karate, but we've already signed up," and "I'm sorry soccer has been so hard for you. I know you'll be glad when the season is over." This lets your child know that while you won't let him quit, at least you understand how he feels.

After all, kids go into activities with excitement and enthusiasm, which lasts until the first bump in the road. Then, kids have to make a decision: *Is the time and effort required to become good really worth it?* To some kids it is. To others, it's not. Regardless, when you're used to things coming easily, it's hard to manage the frustration when things are difficult.

Motivated Smart Kids

Some smart kids will want to take academics to the highest level. They'll start talking about college in elementary school, and even about going to Harvard one day. As a parent, this is exciting. Seeing your child interested in something on a grand scale lets you know your child is not only smart, but also motivated. However, when your child talks about college and future employment, it's important to listen while not appearing to be the driving force. Because smart kids are easily bored and will change their minds; if you attach too much importance to his conversation about Harvard, it may end up pushing your child away.

It's also important not to be the one to start conversations about grand accomplishments. If he wants to tell you about his desire to go to an Ivy League school, say, "That's great. I hope you can go there someday." That's a much different response than, "You're going to have to get straight A's from here on out. Do you know how many applicants that school gets?" The first one is supportive. The second one is loaded with expectations. When you support your child, you allow him to figure out where he fits without deciding for him. When you expect your child to do something, you narrow the playing field and put pressure on him to either fail or succeed in a specific area.

When he asks your opinion about going to Harvard, say, "I'll be happy wherever you go." Many smart kids will get rejected from Harvard, and while you appreciate your child's drive and motivation, you also want to set the tone of *I'll love you regardless*. Smart kids sometimes don't handle rejection well, and it's comforting for them to know they'll have support no matter what.

The Unmotivated Smart Child

Many parents are in the opposite position. They realize how smart their child is but can't seem to get him to take advantage of his opportunities. They see he has a 146 IQ but is doing only grade-level math. According to the Weschler Intelligence Scale, children who score above a 130 are considered to have "very superior" intelligence. Children who score between 120–129 are considered "superior," and those scoring between 110–119 are considered "high average." Average intelligence is considered to be between 90–109, so when a child scores a 146, the expectations are much higher.

If you have a child with a high IQ who is doing only average in school, just be patient. A lot of pressure goes along with being smart. In the early grades (K–2), smart kids have to do next to nothing to stay afloat. Once third grade hits, school gets harder, and smart kids have to try, often creating issues. Trying is not something smart kids are used to. For them, it's like putting on a three-piece suit when you're used to running around in your underwear. It feels heavy, confining, and stuffy, and all you want to do is peel it off, but you can't. Instead, you're stuck trying to find the freedom you used to have.

This is a tough place to be for a smart child: realizing that learning isn't always easy and that life takes effort. He can no longer just slide by; now there are expectations and work to be done to meet these expectations. "Your child can do this," is often what teachers say to the parents of smart kids. "He just doesn't apply himself."

How to Motivate Smart Kids

If your child is unmotivated, start by not blaming him. Think of the things you're unmotivated to do: housework, errands, exercise, balancing your checkbook, filing your taxes, and then think of how you get yourself to do them. You tell yourself: *I'll feel better when this is over.*

That's exactly how you teach smart kids to try. You say, "I know you don't like doing your homework, but when you're finished, we're going to go to the park." That's so much more effective than saying, "You HAVE to do homework. That's just part of life. Do you want to fail third grade?"

That approach is overwhelming to kids. After all, they didn't choose to be smart. Now they're being held to a higher bar than other kids their age, and they see it as unfair. Regardless of kids' immediate desires, it's important for parents to help their kids reach their potential. Letting them waste their intelligence is not a good outcome for anyone. So learning how to motivate them is key.

You can motivate smart kids by:

1. *Empathizing*
2. *Rewarding*

Empathizing is just saying, "I get it. I get that you don't like school. I get that you despise homework. I get that you're bored. I get that all you want to do is play with Lego Star Wars. I get that you hate every minute school is in session and that all you think about is what you're going to do after. I get it. But you have to go because that's the law. I'm sorry."

Rewarding is saying, "You did something you didn't want to do;

now you can do something you do want to do." This is a great life lesson. There are so many things in life we don't want to do, but we do them anyway. We work hard on weekdays so we can go to the lake on weekends. We get up early to go to the gym so we can have dessert after dinner. We make sacrifices every day, and teaching kids that the product of sacrifice is reward is essential to their growth and development.

For smart kids, it's important to do the hard things first. Homework should be done before play. Studying should be finished before their favorite show comes on, and work should be completed before downtime. Some parents choose to let their kids relax for a while after school, and if that works for you, that's fine. Just don't let the fun be so much fun that they can't pull themselves away. If so, they will become even more resentful of school. If they're really into playing outside or building a Lego tower, chances are, getting homework done is going to be even more of a challenge.

How Intelligence Is Valued in the Home

How you view the Seven Types of Intelligence will affect what your child does/does not value. If you are an academic person, you likely value Logical-Mathematical Intelligence. If you are an artist, you likely value Visual-Spatial Intelligence, and if you are an athlete, you likely value Bodily-Kinesthetic Intelligence. This is true even if you never say this to your child. You may never say: "I want you to be a doctor," but if you are a doctor, then your child is going to see becoming a doctor as success. If you are an artist and your child comes home with a winning art project, he's going to see that as more important than an A on a math assignment, because he knows that's what you value.

A friend of mine became an orthopedic surgeon because, growing up, his father used to talk about how amazing the town orthopedic surgeon was. He recalls sitting around the dinner table, hearing his father talk about how smart the orthopedic surgeon was and how much money he made, and although the father never pushed his son to become one, the tone in the house suggested that orthopedic surgeons were the thing to be. My friend was a natural athlete and loved football; however, he chose the academic route because that was what was valued in his home. Forty years later, he's spent his life becoming not what he wanted to be, but what his father wanted him to be.

This lack of awareness of how our parents' values determine our own values is common for the majority of adults. As kids, we did what we thought would be accepted by our parents. I was a basketball player because that's what was valued in my home. Was it my most natural ability? No, but the rewards for doing well in sports were greater than doing well in academics. It wasn't until I acquired a stomach virus during my junior year in college that I finally chose another area to focus on. Sitting on the bench for the first time in my life, I realized that basketball was no longer serving me. I dove into my studies and realized my talents were much greater in academics than they were in sports.

There may be instances when your child will become interested in something you do not value. This doesn't mean your child doesn't value your opinion; it's just that he's found value in his own thing. If you value academics and your child would rather throw a football than do homework, your values are going to collide. You may reward him for getting good grades, but eventually, being a high school quarterback is going to mean more to him than getting a 30 on the ACT. While neither being the quarterback nor scoring a 30 on the ACT guarantees success in life, it's hard to change what a child values, especially if he's getting affirmation for it from his peers. Peer affirmation will nearly always trump parental affirmation, especially as kids get older.

While you shouldn't hide your values from your kids, it's important to consider what comes naturally to your child. If your child has high Logical-Mathematical skills, then valuing academics is going to be in alignment with him. If he has high Bodily-Kinesthetic Intelligence, then valuing sports is going to be a good fit as well.

And if your child has high motivation as well as a natural ability, the sky is the limit on how successful he can be. If he is both smart and motivated in school, he can go to a top university. If he has amazing speed and trains every day, he can become a track star. It's just that motivation and natural abilities don't always align.

Sometimes your child will have the drive but not the natural ability. Other times, he'll have the natural ability but not the drive. When I refer to "drive" I am referring to the passion, discipline, and desire to be great at something. Many anxious kids have a lot of drive and are looking for a way to channel it. Therefore, when they find an outlet, such as sports, music, or theater, they throw all of their energy into becoming great. It's no wonder many famous people have admitted to struggling with anxiety. They had both the drive and a natural ability in a specific area.

How Intelligence Is Valued at School

No matter what you value at home, Logical-Spatial, Lingustic, and Interpersonal Intelligences are what's valued at school. That your child is a great artist, a great athlete, or a great violinist is generally not as important as how well your child reads, does math problems, writes essays, and behaves inside the classroom. Logical-Spatial and Linguistic Intelligences are valued at school because that's what is being tested. That's what teachers are held accountable for, what standardized tests are based on, what's covered on the SAT, and what determines where your child goes to college. If your child does well in these areas, the work itself will not be an issue. Other aspects of life at school might be an issue, but your child will have no problem learning the material he is supposed to master.

Interpersonal Intelligence determines how well your child behaves inside the classroom: how well he gets along with peers, how he responds to teachers, and how he carries himself throughout the school day are extremely important, especially when there are deficiencies in this area. If your child is disruptive, you will get a phone call faster than if your child is struggling academically. If your child is an angel, his learning issues might be overlooked because of his sweet demeanor.

When I was a classroom teacher and saw a student quietly working, I assumed he knew how to do the assignment. If another student was tapping his pencil loudly on his desk, I assumed he didn't know how to do the assignment or couldn't concentrate enough to complete it. The two kids may have had the same issue, but the child tapping the pencil got my attention faster because he was disrupting the other students.

Kids who have a high Interpersonal Intelligence are either loved by teachers who find them enjoyable to be around or disliked because of their tendency to focus on the social aspects of school instead of the schoolwork itself. Kids who have high levels of Interpersonal Intelligence are often big talkers and find socializing to be of utmost importance. I was the child who got the "talks too much" note on every report card, and little did I know that learning how to talk to whomever I was sitting by would help me in my career as a therapist. The tendency to talk to anyone was seen as a bad thing at school but has served as a great asset in my professional life.

While you need to value what your child's school values, focusing too much on it is overwhelming to children. Because Logical-Spatial, Linguistic, and Interpersonal Intelligences are already the focus of so much at school, kids become frustrated and resistant if you continue that focus at home. Especially if school is not going well, talking about it at home only promotes anxiety.

If kids have to rehash something that happened at school, they will not only resent school, they'll resent their time at home. In this case, their behavior at school may bleed over into everything else. School, instead of lasting just seven hours, will end up lasting for twelve or fourteen hours, because kids will spend the whole evening in trouble. However, the main problem with rehashing events that happened at school is that kids often don't remember exactly what happened. They may not remember why they talked out at 9:30, or how they managed to get put out in the hallway. Asking them why they did something they barely remember is not only unfair to them, it's unfair to you. If you can't get the answer you need from your child, it may be better to set up a conference with his teacher than to try and pull information out of your child.

Providing After-School Outlets

A better approach is to focus on the other areas of intelligence during after-school hours. Some kids wait all day for school to be over. They don't enjoy it and live for those few hours in between school and bedtime when they feel successful. Allowing them this time is a wonderful gift to give to a child. Kids need to experiment with the other types of intelligence by taking art classes, doing gymnastics, taking piano lessons, or joining a soccer team.

Finding meaningful activities also helps smart kids control their anxiety. A symptom of anxiety is being "keyed up," and giving kids a chance to release some of that keyed-up energy helps them become less anxious overall. Providing physical outlets, such as Run Fast! Jump High! (Tool #13), is a way to do this. Even if they don't provide a physical release, it is important for anxious kids to be actively engaged in activities they feel positive about. For example, if a child is worried about a math test on Friday, he can go to his favorite art class after school on Thursday. Instead of worrying about the math test, for that hour of creating art, he can feel happy and positive, which will help release some of the anxious energy.

If you have tried several activities and nothing has seemed to stick, it's important not to give up. Activities such as rock climbing, lacrosse, and horseback riding are options that many kids really enjoy. It's also great to have your child do something in the community, such as volunteering at the food bank or helping out with younger children. Community activities help kids feel good about themselves and give them a sense of purpose. One child I worked with was not athletic but really loved animals. Instead of going through another dreadful soccer season, his mom signed him up to be a volunteer at an animal shelter. The child loved it! He formed positive relationships with the animals and couldn't wait to go back every week.

What Giftedness Means to Kids

Giftedness is the term schools use to identify kids who have heightened levels of Logical-Mathematical and Linguistic Intelligence. If you have a child who is certified gifted, then your child has scored 126 or more on the Stanford-Binet Intelligence test, along with scoring in the 90th percentile on a statewide achievement test. Your child may not have been tested yet, as the testing process for giftedness varies widely from state to state. Some children get identified as early as preschool, while other children don't begin the process until third or fourth grade. If your child has received certification for giftedness, then he is among the three million other kids who are currently labeled as gifted in the United States. Each year, programs such as Child Find conduct annual screenings in public schools to determine unidentified gifted students. When I was a school counselor, we identified a boy with a 149 IQ through Child Find who wasn't considered smart by his teachers. He did average work and didn't appear to be listening, yet he scored in the superior range.

The public school system often pulls kids out of the classroom for enrichment classes if they meet the criteria for giftedness. While this can seem like a privilege, leaving the classroom can be tough on kids. Childhood is a time where kids are striving to fit in, and anything that makes a child feel "different" can have negative effects. When gifted kids are pulled out, they not only miss what goes on in the classroom, but also have to explain where they have been. Saying they're in a program for smart kids can have social consequences, so they will often just call it a "group" or a "program" to avoid drawing more attention to themselves.

If your child goes to a private school, you may not know if your child meets the criteria for giftedness. Private schools are not required by law to provide services for gifted children (or any child with a special need), and many do not actively seek out smart kids for gifted screenings. Parents can have their own testing conducted, or they can ask the school to provide testing—although they may not agree. For bright kids at private schools, parents are often expected to seek out their own resources to help challenge their child.

I've worked with many kids who have scored in the 140s or 150s on intelligence tests and have no idea how smart they are. Their parents have wisely chosen not to tell them about their scores and instead have encouraged them just to do their best. If your child has produced a high IQ score, I would recommend this same approach. After all, giftedness is an adult word; kids have no use for it. The only thing giftedness means to kids is they get to go to a different class (sometimes) and do extra work (occasionally). What being "gifted" really means to kids is that school is easy and, too often, boring.

Gifted kids often finish their work early and spend most of their time reading. If they have a good teacher, they'll do extra work, finish that too, and then spend more time reading. Their boredom often leads to trouble once they run out of reading material. They'll start talking or drawing or disturbing the class. They'll correct their teacher when she slips up. And it's no surprise that school, instead of being their comfort zone, can become a dreaded place. For children who excel in types of intelligence besides those identified by gifted programs, school can be especially tough, because they experience such a discrepancy between success and failure.

What do I mean by that? If your child is a brilliant artist, he will feel great measures of success when he goes to art class. An hour later, when he's called on to read a short story, he stutters, feels embarrassed, and suddenly his success in art class, only an hour before, has completely vanished. The same goes for kids who excel in sports. In P.E., they score the winning shot in a basketball game and are celebrated. They are on cloud nine when they reenter the classroom, only to find out they failed yesterday's math test and have to take it again. This discrepancy is confusing for kids. They were smart enough to elude two defenders and score the winning basket but not smart enough to add 6 + 8.

If your child is not getting enough stimulation at school, you may need to find other ways to provide the level of stimulation he needs. If he's not being stimulated academically, you can enroll him in programs such as Kumon (www.kumon.com), which provides an individualized math and reading curriculum for each child based on his abilities, not his age or grade level. For example, if your child is in third grade but is capable of doing sixth-grade math, Kumon will provide a curriculum of sixth-grade math, so your child will not only be challenged, but also will be able to make even more gains in math.

If your child is an amazing artist but isn't being challenged by the school's art program, you can enroll him in art classes based on his level of talent. You can request private lessons from an artist or make a special request for your child to be in a community-based class with older students, based on his ability. The same goes for kids who have musical talents. Finding a voice coach or a violin teacher who will allow your child to maximize his gifts will often give smart kids the stimulation they need. Finding the right teacher is imperative, and once you find someone who can connect with your child and invest in his talent, smart kids will often grow exponentially.

What You Must Remember...

The ability to take concepts and ideas to the next level is not a choice; it is something smart kids do without trying. While this skill can be a great asset in school, sports, art, or everyday life, it can also cause great pain. Because smart kids are always thinking, their minds never rest. They are constantly spinning thoughts over and over, which can help them be brilliant and creative but can also lead to a continual struggle with anxiety.

2

Understanding Your Child's Anxiety

• •

I f you look up "anxiety" in the *DSM (Diagnostic and Statistical Manual of Mental Health Disorders)* you will find there are six types of anxiety:

- Generalized Anxiety Disorder (GAD)
- Social Phobia
- Panic Disorder
- Specific Phobia
- Post-Traumatic Stress Disorder (PTSD)
- Obsessive-Compulsive Disorder (OCD)

Each type has a number of symptoms and a time frame for which the anxiety has been present, which is often six months. The six-month time frame protects people from being diagnosed with anxiety disorders when, in fact, they are just experiencing a bump in the road. Many kids will experience a brief period of anxiety that lasts only a few weeks or months, while others will experience ongoing anxiety throughout their childhood. If your child has experienced intense anxiety for even a week, you may be concerned about your

Types of Anxiety

Generalized Anxiety Disorder (GAD): Excessive, unrealistic worry and tension, even if there is little or nothing to provoke the anxiety.

Social Anxiety Disorder: Overwhelming worry and self-consciousness about everyday social situations. The worry often centers on a fear of being judged by others, or behaving in a way that might cause embarrassment or lead to ridicule.

Panic Disorder: Feelings of terror that strike suddenly and repeatedly with no warning. Other symptoms of a panic attack include sweating, chest pain, palpitations (irregular heartbeats), and a feeling of choking.

Specific Phobias: Intense fear of objects or situations, such as snakes, heights, or flying. The level of fear is usually inappropriate to the situation and may cause the person to avoid common, everyday situations.

Post-Traumatic Stress Disorder (PTSD): Can develop following a traumatic and/or terrifying event, such as the unexpected death of a loved one or a natural disaster. People with PTSD often have lasting and frightening thoughts and memories of the event and tend to be emotionally numb.

Obsessive-Compulsive Disorder (OCD): Constant thoughts or fears that cause people to perform certain rituals or routines. The disturbing thoughts are called obsessions, and the rituals are called compulsions. An example is a person with an unreasonable fear of germs who constantly washes his or her hands.

child having an anxiety disorder. But whether your child does have a diagnosable anxiety disorder or not, for the purpose of this book, I feel it's important to help kids with their fears. No matter how long it's been, the fear is real, and as a parent, it's important to understand your child's fears and what you can do to help.

When I sit down with parents, I help them understand their child's fears on a larger scale. Instead of simply diagnosing their child with one type of anxiety according to the *DSM*, I help parents understand what kinds of things are triggering their child and how to help them manage their fears. To help them understand their child's fears better, I simplify and break anxiety down into two main categories: *Object-Oriented* and *Relational*. This helps parents get a better sense of their child's triggers and helps them prepare him for fearful situations in a simple way.

Object-Oriented Anxiety in Kids

Kids with Object-Oriented Anxiety have debilitating fears of storms, getting kidnapped, going to the doctor, getting shots, getting hurt, and of someone breaking into their home. They are constantly checking with their outside environment: looking at the sky for clouds, listening for intruders, and identifying strangers in the grocery store parking lot.

Kids with Object-Oriented Anxiety are also drawn to watching the news. They pay attention to the weather report, acts of terrorism, wars around the globe, and the house that was broken into right down the street. They want to know how tornadoes happen and if a tsunami will hit the same beach they'll be visiting for summer vacation. They do online research about diseases, natural disasters, and how to get rid of head lice—just in case they have it.

The ultimate goal for a child with Object-Oriented Anxiety is to be free from harm. Until the storm passes, the doctor's appointment ends, the sun comes up without anyone breaking in, the child with Object-Oriented Anxiety will feel unsafe. The problem with this is that life doesn't give kids the chance to be free from harm. There is always the threat of weather or dangerous people or a fire suddenly breaking out. Without some intervention, children with Object-Oriented Anxiety will be keyed up and fearful most of the time.

Helping Kids with Object-Oriented Anxiety

As a therapist, I teach kids their own tools to use during anxious moments. I will go into the tools more in detail in Part Two, but for example, I teach kids with Object-Oriented Anxiety how to do Square Breathing (Tool #1) in the midst of fear. I teach them how to focus their attention on positive thoughts by Changing the Channel (Tool #3).

Because kids with Object-Oriented Anxiety aren't usually worried about how they are perceived, I also help them to refrain from acting in inappropriate ways in public—to manage their emotions instead. Kids with Object-Oriented Anxiety have no qualms about making a scene in the grocery store. They don't care about making a scene at school either, and will cling to their parents, scream, yell, and curl up into a ball in the hallway. Whatever they feel, they will do. As a parent of a child with Object-Oriented Anxiety, you will be more worried about how your child behaves than he is. He doesn't see what the big deal is if he holds on to your leg while you drag him to his classroom, or if he rips the curtain off the van window while you take him to a soccer game he doesn't want to go to.

That's why it's important to teach kids with Object-Oriented Anxiety that social norms need to be followed. Just because social norms aren't a big deal to them doesn't mean they should be ignored. In the long run, if kids act out in public, their reputation will be affected. Other kids don't easily forget those who've been dragged out of the classroom, who cling to their parents, or who throw a fit in the pick-up line.

For kids who experience high levels of Object-Oriented Anxiety, managing these fears can be difficult. If they are afraid of storms, they may rock back and forth and cover their eyes until the storm ends. If they are deathly afraid of tornadoes, they may have a stomachache when they hear the sirens or feel panic in their bodies.

Once the storm ends or the sirens turn off, these anxious kids will often go through a period of readjusting back into the emotional state they were in before the anxiety-producing event. This can happen rather quickly, or it can take up to several hours. Recalibrating is important, and it allows anxious kids to feel safe again.

Relational Anxiety in Kids

Kids with Relational Anxiety worry about people. They overfocus on friendships, how much attention little brother is getting, and what other people think of them. If they think someone doesn't like them, they are hyperaware of it, often confusing a look that meant nothing to mean someone despises them. Kids with Relational Anxiety also take in enormous amounts of information about other people. They notice what other people are wearing, how they are acting, and what signals they're giving off. They pay attention to who's friends with whom, what is "normal" and "not normal," and are careful to stay within the limits. They worry about whom they're going to sit with at the birthday party, what someone will think of their new haircut, and how much their teacher likes them. Kids with Relational Anxiety are always aware of how they are seen by others.

When everyone likes them, they have plenty of friends, and little brother is at summer camp, things are perfect for a child with Relational Anxiety. But it's a delicate balancing act that can be thrown off very easily. The day is going great until someone makes a snide comment or until they aren't invited to the birthday party, and then everything crashes.

Until balance is regained, the life of a Relationally Anxious child can be tough. They will worry about the party, the friend, or the event until the issue has passed or until things are resolved with that person. Equilibrium will then be regained until the next event involving people triggers another surge of anxiety.

Helping Kids with Relational Anxiety

Kids with Relational Anxiety are the opposite of kids with Object-Oriented Anxiety. They care too much about what other people think. They try to hide their weaknesses and are devastated if anyone outside of the family knows about their behavior. They have just as many tantrums as kids with Object-Oriented Anxiety, but they don't want anyone outside of their family to know about them. They'll throw a fit in the car on the way to school, but when they step out of the car, they'll act calm and collected. They'll pretend a hurtful remark made by a friend was no big deal until they get home and burst into tears.

Because kids with Relational Anxiety work so hard at keeping appearances, they are often doubly hard to deal with at home. They stuff all of their emotions inside, only to come home and explode. Home is where their anxiety comes out, because home is where their safe people are. The definition of a safe person is someone who will accept them no matter what. A safe parent is a valuable resource to a child with Relational Anxiety. After he's spent all day fearing rejection, he can come home to an environment where he knows he'll be accepted.

The overall goal for a child with Relational Anxiety is to learn how to integrate the two sides of himself: the person at home with the person at school. Because there's such a stark difference between the two, kids with Relational Anxiety can become confused about who they really are. They see themselves as leaders at school but troublemakers at home. They see themselves as capable at school but incapable at home. This only makes things more difficult at home, because they begin searching for reasons for why things are going so poorly there. They may blame their annoying brother or the broccoli on their dinner plate instead of realizing neither is really the problem. They are simply letting all of their emotions out, looking for something to blame for how bad they feel. A great way to improve the home environment for kids with Relational Anxiety is to implement a reward system, such as The Marble System (Tool #6). This helps them become successful at home and more able to integrate the two parts of themselves.

Anxiety Triggers

Anxiety triggers are what cause your child's anxiety to flare up. Knowing what triggers your child's anxiety gives you 80 percent of the information you need to help your child. The other 20 percent is knowing which tools to use to help your child get through their anxious periods, and we'll get to that in Part Two.

We all get triggered by certain things, whether it is work or money or our irritating friend who won't stop calling during a crisis. When I work with kids, I call these triggers **Feelings Buttons**, but as adults we have them too. It's just that we're more aware (or at least should be) of which situations trigger our anxiety and why.

If your son's anxiety is triggered by social situations, it's important to keep that in mind before dropping him off at the birthday party. You may also want to implement a tool, such as Giving Your Child a Role (Tool #7) to help your child navigate the social situation. If your daughter's anxiety is triggered by storms, it might be a good idea to check the weather before driving to the beach for vacation. It's not that you should avoid taking your child to the birthday party or the beach, it's just that you should be tuned in to your child's triggers enough to be prepared for a strong reaction if things don't go perfectly.

In handling these strong reactions, try to stay as relaxed as possible. On the way to the birthday party, refrain from asking, "Are you okay?" or saying, "You're going to be fine." Instead, make sure you are calm and in a neutral emotional state. If your child wants to talk about his fears, that's fine; just don't be the one to bring them up. Instead, talk about something not related to the event. Changing the Channel (Tool #3) is a great way to change the conversation to a fun activity that's coming up or a vacation he's looking forward to.

If your child becomes angry and starts lashing out, try to emotionally disengage. That doesn't mean you disengage from your child completely, but it does mean you refrain from escalating to your child's level of frustration. While every parent has limits and can only take so much, try to stay neutral as long as possible. Listen to what your child is saying, and acknowledge his feelings. Instead of trying to change the way he thinks about the event, say, "I know you're scared. I wish I could make it better for you."

If you try to make it better by saying, "You're going to have a great time," you'll get resistance, because your child is not in a rational place. Trying to rationalize with an irrational person never works. Plus, children want to bring you down to their emotional state. If they're angry, they want you to be angry too, but going there with them only causes more problems. Instead, stay empathetic and neutral while allowing your child to release his anxiety.

Also, keep in mind that when anxious kids are triggered, they may bring up issues from the past. Emotions are a lot like spaghetti—they cling together—so when kids get upset about one thing, they tend to get upset about everything. On the way to an anxiety-producing event, they might bring up a disagreement with a sibling. They will talk about how awful the event went the last time you made them go and how you always make them do things they don't want to do. Be careful to not engage in these types of discussions with your child. Be sure to listen and acknowledge their feelings, but don't try to put out fires. Saying, "You chose to go to that event, not me," will only make things worse.

Default Worries

Default Worries are the worries kids go back to over and over again. Just when you think your child is finally over his fear of storms, he'll see a grey cloud and go into a panic. After you think he's gotten over his fear of death, he'll tug on your shoulder at 3:00 a.m., saying he's afraid you're going to die. While this is exhausting for you as a parent, there are good reasons why kids use Default Worries. Here are the two main reasons:

1. **Kids have no idea why they're feeling anxious.**

   There are times when anxious kids have no idea why they're worried. It's 2:00 in the morning, their heart is racing, and their stomach is upset. Nothing *appears* to be going wrong, yet they can't sleep, and they can't slow their mind down. During these times, anxious kids will use Default Worries as a way to make sense of how they're feeling. This is a basic survival instinct—to understand why you feel the way you do—so kids will draw on a worry they've had before and view it as the current reason for the way they feel.

   A parent's first reaction to this is: *Oh no! It's back!* Not to fear. The worry will probably go away and come back again periodically. What *is* important is that your child is afraid right now. Don't panic, and don't try to rack your brain for something that will remove the fear forever. Just be there with him and ride it out.

2. **They are trying to burn off excess mental energy.**

   Anxious kids have lots of mental energy. Their minds are always running, and when they don't have anything to focus on, they will choose a Default Worry to burn off the excess energy. It's just like when you play with your iPhone in the waiting room of a doctor's appointment. You have nothing better to do, so you scan through your phone, looking for a way to kill time. That's much like what anxious kids are doing. They have extra energy, and they need somewhere to put it. If your child has too much time on his hands, try using Structuring the Unstructured (Tool #8). It's a great way to keep kids from gravitating to Default Worries as a way to release their mental energy.

Common Default Worries		
Death	Doctor's Appointments	The End/Beginning of School
Getting Sick	Global Warming	Storms
Growing Up	Achievement Tests	Natural Disasters

The worries listed above are what keep the majority of anxious kids trapped in their minds. Growing up, getting sick, and dying are three inevitable parts of life and can keep an anxious kid's mind occupied for years. There are no specific solutions for these worries, so kids spin the scenarios through their minds in search of possible solutions. They'll think about what it would be like if you died, if they died, or if their dog died. Because they're smart, they realize that any of those scenarios are possible.

If your child worries about death, don't try to make him feel better by assuring him he won't die or you won't die. Instead, acknowledge his feelings by saying, "I'm sorry you're so worried about this. I wish I could make it better for you." When you approach his fear this way, you are connecting and supporting him without making promises about something you have no control over.

Doctor's appointments, achievement tests, and the beginning and ending of school are yearly events many anxious kids dread. There is no escaping them either, so anxious kids can pull them out and worry about them at any given time. Storms, natural disasters, and global warming are also fears anxious kids can draw on. They are all over the news, and there's no sure way of knowing if or when they will happen. If you live in a part of the country where there are lots of storms, anxious kids will worry about that. If you have earthquakes, forest fires, or torrential rains, anxious kids will choose to worry about what is covered most on the local news or talked about by peers and classmates. It takes just one kid to say "My mom almost got caught in that tornado last week" to make an anxious kid worry about tornadoes for months.

Baits

While anxiety triggers are what cause your child's anxiety to flare up, baits are what your child uses to empty his emotional tank. Baits and triggers are different. Baits are not what trigger your child's anxiety, but instead, what he uses to release his emotions. For example, if your child is worried about going to the dentist, he might bait you into an argument about putting on his pajamas. Putting on his pajamas isn't one of his triggers, but because he is worried about going to the dentist, he will bait you into an argument so he can release some of his anxiety.

After a long day, when kids are tired and they haven't gotten their needs met, they will often bait parents into arguments to let out some of their emotions. Suddenly, the bathwater is too cold, the food is too salty, the toothbrush too hard. It's important to see the outburst for what it is—an emptying of the emotional tank—and for what it is not—something you necessarily need to respond to. You can adjust the bath temperature all night long...they're still not going to like it.

When you are feeling baited, step back and ask yourself three questions:

1. *Is my child hungry?*
2. *Is my child tired?*
3. *Is my child sick?*

If your answer is "yes" to any of these three questions, then your child is not in Rational Mind.

Rational Mind is when your child is able to think through a decision. He has the ability to say, "If I refuse to take a bath, I'm going to get in trouble," and decide it's not worth it. If your child is not in Rational Mind, he either won't go through the decision-making process or simply won't care. He'll continue to fight about the bath until his emotional tank is drained or until he finds another outlet that will do the draining for him.

If your answer is "no" to the above three questions, then you are likely dealing with an emotional issue, or for the purposes of this book, an anxiety issue. Children with anxiety will bait parents to release their emotions, and this often leads to a meltdown. When children melt down, they actually leave the situation feeling better, whereas adults leave the situation feeling worse.

After a meltdown, children feel better because they are no longer spinning with emotion. Their bodies relax, their minds rest, and they feel equilibrium again. Once they feel better, they might apologize or be confused by their actions. "I don't know why I did that," is what many anxious kids say after a meltdown, and the truth is, they don't. They're completely unaware of why they handled the situation like they did. They had no idea their emotional tank was full and needed draining. All they felt was a surge of emotion.

If this is typical for your child, please refer to the *Think Sheet* in the back of the book. *Think Sheets* help children process behavior instead of allowing them to simply apologize and move on. After a child has calmed down, either have the child fill out the sheet on his own or go over it orally with him so you can wrap up the event and both move on.

Anxiety and Sensitivity

Many anxious kids are also highly sensitive. If you haven't read *The Highly Sensitive Child* by Elaine Aron, I would recommend it. Years ago, we called Highly Sensitive Kids "dramatic," but now we're learning that sensitivity is not a choice; it's just the way some kids are made. When I talk to parents about their child's anxiety, some will also report their child's sensitivity to clothing, noises, changes in schedule, and touch. "Is this anxiety?" they often ask. The answer is that there are very few situations when it is just anxiety. It's often anxiety and Attention Deficit Hyperactivity Disorder (ADHD); anxiety and Attention Deficit Disorder (ADD); anxiety and sensory issues; or in this case, anxiety and sensitivity.

When talking about sensitivity, Judith Orloff, a psychiatrist and author of *Emotional Freedom*, said: "It's like feeling something with fifty fingers as opposed to ten. You have more receptors to perceive things." A Harvard psychologist, Jerome Kagan, found that about 10 to 20 percent of infants begin life with a tightly tuned nervous system that makes them easily aroused, jumpy, and distressed in response to novel stimuli. Such highly reactive infants, as he termed them, run the risk of growing into "inhibited" children, who tend to withdraw from experience as a defense and are at high risk for anxiety.

Brain-imaging studies show that the reactivity of highly sensitive people reflects a distinctive biological feature: a hyperresponsive amygdala. The amygdala is the brain center that assesses threats and governs the fear response. The amygdala is what keeps anxious kids on the constant lookout for danger. Kagan believes Highly Sensitive People are unusually susceptible to both emotional and tangible irritants—for example, mean-spirited comments, as well as pollen or dander in the air.

If your child is highly sensitive, he will respond to things very differently than other kids. He may also process anxiety very differently. Each child has a different experience with anxiety, and as a parent, it's important to understand how your child processes anxiety. Knowing how he processes his fears and worries will help you know how best to parent him.

3

How Children Process Anxiety and Why It Matters

Parent #1: "He won't talk to me. I know something is wrong, but he denies it. I don't know what to do."

Parent #2: "He won't stop talking about his fears. He asks fifty times a day where I'm going. I can't even go to the bathroom without him knocking on the door asking when I'm coming out."

Both parents have a seven-year-old child. Both parents live on the same street, their kids go to the same school, and their parenting styles are very similar. So why is it that the child of Parent #1 won't talk about his anxiety and the child of Parent #2 won't stop? Because their children are processing anxiety in completely different ways.

The child of Parent #1 is an Inward Processor, so he keeps his fears inside. The child of Parent #2 is an Outward Processor, and he talks about his fears as a means to feel better.

The Ways in Which We Process Emotions

To understand how children process emotions, it's best to understand how we, as adults, process them. Take a few moments and think about your circle of friends:

Think about the friend who calls during a crisis. She needs to talk ASAP, and when you are able to connect, she wants to talk about her problem. She tells you EVERYTHING that's going on, and all of her emotions come out. She cries, she laughs, she yells. She tells you how sad, frustrated, and angry she feels...she expresses it all. She starts at the beginning of the story and takes you through every detail of her emotional process. She doesn't need prompting or advice; it just flows out of her. At some point, she calms down and is ready to hang up the phone. Whether you've had a chance to say anything or not, your friend got what she needed in that you were there to listen. *That friend is an Outward Processor.*

Now think about the friend who becomes distant during a crisis. She withdraws, doesn't seem present, and stops showing up to social functions. She delays returning phone calls and emails, and when you ask how she's doing, she says "Fine" or "I really don't want to talk about it." Not only has she pulled away from you, but she's also pulled away from your other friends too, and it seems like nobody can get her to open up. Then, after some time, she starts coming around again. She accepts a dinner invitation, and with everyone on the edge of their seat, she tells you she's getting a divorce or her son is now at a therapeutic boarding school. She'll be matter-of-fact about it, because by then most of the emotions are gone and she's at a stable place. *This friend is an Inward Processor.*

While you are friends with both of these people, your friendship will change when there is a crisis. With your Outward Processing friend, you might become overwhelmed, because she needs to talk all the time. You might start screening her phone calls because you just don't have time to deal with her problems anymore. With your Inward Processing friend, you might feel hurt and disconnected that she isn't responding to you and may have a hard time settling back into a friendship once her crisis is over.

Now, which one are you?

Are you the type of person who needs to talk about problems, or are you the type of person who prefers just to think about them? When you're upset with your spouse, do you process your feelings as they come up, or do you pull away until your head is clear?

This is important, because the way you process your own emotions is how you'll expect your child to process his. If you are an Inward Processor, you may have a hard time understanding why your Outward Processing child always needs to talk. If you are an Outward Processor, you may have a hard time understanding why your Inward Processing child won't tell you what is going on. You may ask question after question and still not get the response you're looking for.

As a parent, it's important to understand the difference between how you and your child process emotions. If you are an Outward Processor, you may have to stop asking your Inward Processing child questions. You may need to become comfortable with the silence and know that talking is not how your child deals with his emotions. If you are an Inward Processor, you may have to become more patient in listening to your child's problems. Instead of becoming frustrated or jumping to giving advice, you may just have to sit back and listen, because that is what your child really needs. What's most important is that you understand your child's style and allow him the right opportunities to connect with you.

Communicating Negative Emotions vs. Positive Emotions

Before we look further into how kids process emotions, it's important to understand that the way we process negative emotions is often different than how we process everything else. You may be a very chatty person who never seems to stop talking, but when something difficult happens, you either avoid coming to social events or avoid talking about your experiences. Being an outgoing person doesn't automatically make someone an Outward Processor.

The same is true for Inward Processors. Just because someone is quiet doesn't mean they are an Inward Processor. In fact, many quiet people are often Outward Processors. When they're going through a rough time, they have a list of people they can call and talk things over with. They reach out and openly share what's going on with them. They often don't have much use for small talk, so when they call one of their safe people, they immediately get to the point. They share what's happening and feel better after they've talked about it.

Essentially, you can't judge a book by its cover when it comes to the way we process emotions. We all do what comes naturally to us until we are forced to do something different. If we have a spouse that processes differently, we may be forced to learn a different style, but otherwise we'll likely continue processing emotions the same throughout our lives.

How Kids Process Negative Emotions

Children are concrete and egocentric, and they don't have the capacity to gain objectivity on their emotions. Because of their developmental limitations, the way in which kids process emotions is intense and extreme. What happens in their world immediately affects them. What they feel, they feel in huge amounts, and because they're egocentric, they don't understand how their behavior could have a negative effect on someone else.

While adult Outward Processors can take a step back and realize they've been talking for an hour straight, child Outward Processors will just continue talking. They don't realize they've been talking about their worries non-stop or that no one else has had a chance to talk. Their worries are the only things that matter; therefore, until they feel better, they will continue down their path of expressing emotions. If they're afraid of going upstairs, they'll ask, "Will you go up there with me?" twenty times in a row, and if they don't want to go to the sleepover, they'll keep reminding you and reminding you without any awareness that they're repeating.

The same goes for Inward Processors. Adult Inward Processors are smart enough to cancel their social plans while they're having a rough time, because they know they need time to process. They don't need people asking them what's going on with their marriage or why their child got suspended from school. They simply step away and take the time they need to sort things out. Child Inward Processors don't have this option. Because they aren't able to make their own schedules and determine where they go and when, when something is bothering them, they can't escape. If they have siblings, the problem can be even worse. If they go to their room, their sibling will follow. If they say "Leave me alone," their sibling will come even closer. Even if they could have time alone, Inward Processors often let out their emotions in the way that makes them feel the most comfortable: through their behavior.

Let's look at the examples below:

Sam—Inward Processor, Eight Years Old

Sam was a blissful child until his younger sister, Isabel, was born. Until Isabel, he'd had three years of undivided attention from his parents, and when she was born, everything crumbled. Sam went from being happy and joyful to angry and aggressive and began blaming all of his behavior on Isabel. Instead of expressing his jealousy of her, he became aggressive to the point that his parents couldn't trust him to be alone with Isabel. His parents disciplined him for his behavior, so Sam was always in trouble, and Isabel became the "golden child." Sam couldn't express his true feelings about his sister, and his behavior grew so intense that his parents sought counseling for him.

In the initial parent session, Sam's parents described him as being angry, aggressive, and irritable at home, but his teachers had "glowing" things to say about him. His teacher described him as a leader and expressed zero issues about his behavior.

When I first met with Sam, I realized he had no idea how he felt. When we did a feelings activity, he had a very difficult time identifying three feeling cards that reflected his mind-set, out of a stack of twenty-five. After a few sessions, he was able to choose his feelings more easily, but still, he chose only extreme emotions such as angry or excited. Feelings such as jealous, frustrated, and confused were never chosen—he didn't seem to have a handle on more subtle feelings.

Inward Processors often have a hard time identifying subtle feelings. Because their feelings are stuck in their head, they notice only the big ones, such as angry and excited. This is a problem for a child like Sam, whose true feeling was a subtle one—jealousy. He was jealous of his sister, but since jealousy is a subtle emotion, he wasn't recognizing it and instead was expressing it as anger. Jealousy is often the root fear of children with Relational Anxiety, because they are in constant fear of losing their parents' love and attention.

In my work with Sam, I taught him how to identify his jealousy and gave him the tools he needed to manage his anxiety around it. I also taught his mother how to do a Feelings Check-In (Tool #15) on a daily basis to improve his emotional intelligence. To further improve his communication around his emotions, I encouraged Sam to express his feelings through writing notes to his mother. She in turn would write back, expressing her gratitude to him for sharing his emotions. Inward processors tend to communicate better through writing than they do talking. His mother ended up buying a journal that she and Sam passed back and forth for several months, and over time, Sam's behavior began to improve. He learned how to get the positive attention he desperately wanted rather than the negative attention he had gotten in the past.

Jack—Outward Processor, Eight Years Old

Jack began talking at six months and hasn't stopped talking since. He is constantly engaging his parents in conversations and is repeatedly telling them how afraid he is of going to sleepaway camp. He also shares his worries about school and says he may need to talk to a professional because they are getting worse. He's already talked to the school counselor on several occasions and, on the drive home from school, will talk about his day for so long that his mother will have to interrupt him in order for his younger sister to have a chance to talk.

Jack recently watched a cartoon in which a scary creature popped out, and ever since, he has been terrified. He doesn't want to go anywhere in the house alone and is constantly asking his mom where she is. He also has trouble falling asleep and begs to sleep with his parents. When they say "no," he ends up climbing in bed with them in the middle of the night anyway. Jack's parents are exhausted and have no idea what to do.

When I first met with Jack, he walked right in my office and told me why he was there. "I worry a lot, about a lot of things," he said before sitting down. When I asked him to choose his feelings, he easily chose worried, confused, and overwhelmed, because he was having a hard time sleeping, and his worries were getting worse. He went on to choose five more feelings and spent the next fifteen minutes explaining them. This did not surprise me, because Outward Processors are very good at articulating their feelings. Talking about feelings comes naturally to them, and they've usually had lots of practice. While talking about feelings is great, Outward Processors can process their feelings too much, making them more worried than they were before.

In working with Jack, I needed to set boundaries around his worries. He loved sharing his feelings. If I'd only let him share, however, things wouldn't have improved. He needed to learn to what do about his feelings, not just express them. So I helped Jack find the balance between sharing and doing. The sharing was what he was good at; the doing (applying techniques) was what he was not. I also helped Jack's mother learn to set boundaries around his questions by teaching her The Five Question Rule (Tool #4).

Our sessions were structured so that half of our time was spent talking about feelings and the other half was spent on tools. For example, when he expressed feeling overwhelmed, I taught him Brain Plate (Tool #12), which gave him a concrete strategy to help him feel better. If I had just let Jack talk about being overwhelmed, he wouldn't have had the tools to help channel his anxiety. Over time, Jack began to identify what he was feeling and what to do when he felt a certain way. He became empowered, and while he still wanted and needed to talk, he began talking less about negative emotions and more about life in general.

The Separation of Inward Processors

Because Inward Processors tend not to include other people in their processing, parents often feel an emotional separation from their child. Not knowing what is going on with your child is scary, and the reality is, parents of Inward Processors often don't. Their kids may grunt or hiss or growl when they're angry but will refuse to talk about why. When parents try to connect with them at an emotional level, Inward Processors will push them away, leaving their parents to guess what is going on with them.

Within this separation lies a lack of emotional closeness, something every parent wants. Parents want to talk with their kids. They want them to open up, but when their child is pushing them away, parents often become frustrated and give up. Rest assured, pushing you away is not what kids really need; it's just what they're most comfortable with. What they need is to feel connected and loved, but Inward Processors often aren't sure how to do that. So parents try to connect and Inward Processors push them away, creating a seemingly unending cycle of separateness.

The Investment of Outward Processors

What happens with Outward Processors is quite the opposite. Outward Processors are constantly trying to connect with parents to the point that parents begin trying to detach. Outward Processors are always searching for a way to connect, whether that's sharing about their day or expressing their fears. "Hey, Mom," "Hey, Mom," "Hey, Mom" is what the parents of Outward Processors often hear, and at some point, they are so tired of listening and fielding questions that they snap. Since they feel their other kids are not getting the same level of attention, they are forced to set boundaries.

Outward Processors love nothing more than attention, but while Inward Processors will get it through behavior, Outward Processors will get it through words. They will make sure you know how they feel, what they want to do on Saturday, and how you can make their birthday extra special. They will also tell you how badly their friend Kate is treating them and how awful it is making them feel. After hearing about Kate day after day, many parents develop the same level of frustration with Kate that their child has.

This is where the investment comes in. Since your daughter has told you how awful Kate is, you've become invested in her staying away from Kate. You've become angry at Kate yourself and have considered calling her mother to tell her how awful she's being to your daughter. You've also been there to encourage, cheerlead, and give advice, and once your child is finally free of Kate's punishment, she will do the most absurd thing. She will decide to be friends with Kate again! Ugh! After all that, your child wants to be friends with the very person you worked so hard to get her away from. Since you've invested so much time and energy into your child being free of this friend, you feel just as much pain as your child does and can't figure out why she would subject herself to the same ridicule again.

This is a hard position for a parent to be in, because your emotions have come from an honest place. You wanted nothing more than for your child to have positive friendships, but you got sucked into the drama. You joined in with your child to the point where you stayed awake at night, thinking about Kate, and now you feel silly for having an agenda against a nine-year-old. So you bite your tongue and hope your daughter makes a different choice, but regardless, you will never feel the same about Kate. You have too much emotion invested. This affects Outward Processing children, because your investment can keep your child from resolving the conflict. She may think she's not supposed to be friends with Kate and suffer social consequences because of it. If she decides to resolve the conflict with Kate, she'll likely expect you to be on board. When you're not, she may say, "I thought I was supposed to be friends with everybody! That's what my teacher said."

Inward vs. Outward Processing: Is it Hardwired or Learned?

Common sense may tell you that if you openly share emotions with your kids, they will become Outward Processors. There are countless books and lots of research about parenting styles and how to help kids express their emotions freely. However simple this may seem, I sit with high-functioning, emotionally open parents everyday whose children won't talk to them. They've tried modeling, they've tried asking, and have resorted to pulling teeth. Still, their kids won't open up.

What I've found is that the way children process emotions is more wired than learned. My childhood home wasn't filled with hours of open expression, yet I was a natural talker, and I became an Outward Processor, like my sister. Ultimately, I am an Outward Processor who was raised by two Inward Processors (who also raised another Inward Processor, in my brother!).

A Deeper Understanding

Let's take a deeper look at the differences between Inward and Outward Processors and how to connect with them in a meaningful way. The chart below lists the main differences.

Inward Processor	Outward Processor
Solve problems by thinking	Solve problems by talking
Communicate through behavior	Communicate through words
Deny feelings	Exaggerate feelings
Blame others	Blame themselves

As you can see, Inward Processors and Outward Processors are on opposite ends of the spectrum. They handle situations differently, both in their minds and in their actions. Let's look at their differences more closely by examining:

- How they solve problems
- How they communicate
- How they deal with feelings
- How they handle blame

How They Solve Problems

Inward Processors solve problems internally. They think their way through problems and come up with a solution without the help of others. It's not that they intend to shut people out, it's just that shutting people out works best for them. They are comfortable with the voice in their head and uncomfortable with that voice being heard by others. Until they sort it out, they don't want to communicate. It might take a day, a week, or a month, but at the end of an anxiety cycle, Inward Processors will have come up with a solution on their own.

Outward Processors solve problems externally. When an anxious thought pops into their mind, they will tell the safest person, usually a parent, and don't stop talking about it until their fear goes away. If they are extremely worried about something, they will talk incessantly about their fear. Even when solutions are suggested, anxious kids will be resistant to try them. The process of verbalizing fears is what Outward Processors are looking for, more than a solution to their problem. For that reason, when you try to give an Outward Processor a solution, they will dismiss it or even argue with you that it won't work. Offering solutions shuts down their process, so until they have calmed down enough to gain perspective, it's best to just listen. Once they have regrouped, you can offer suggestions, but generally Outward Processors will talk long enough to figure things out on their own.

How They Communicate

Inward Processors communicate through behavior. This is very important to remember: It's not that Inward Processors don't communicate, it's just that they communicate by showing instead of by telling. The way they "show" their anxiety depends on the child. Some children show their anxiety through disruptive behavior. Because their emotional tank is full, the littlest things set them off. They won't tell you they're worried about going to the dentist, but instead will start yelling in the car on the way to the dentist appointment. They don't tell you they are afraid of performing at the piano recital, but they pick a fight with their sister the day before the event.

For the children who aren't disruptive, they will "show" you their anxiety by becoming distant. They may pull away, seem distracted, and choose not to participate in activities they usually enjoy. Even when you ask them what's wrong, they won't tell you. Instead, they process their emotions in their head until they've sorted things out.

At the other end of the spectrum, Outward Processors have no problem with communication. They will tell you how worried, scared, angry, and jealous they are, even when you don't ask. They will talk about how sad they are about not getting invited to the birthday party or how scared they are of getting struck by a tornado, and they won't stop talking until the issue is resolved.

After the issue is resolved, the Outward Processor will move on to something else. Parenting an Outward Processor is challenging for this reason. As we've talked about, Outward Processors flood parents with worries about one specific issue, "hooking" their parent into becoming emotionally invested, and then move on to another worry. So just when their parents get them off the soccer team, they say they are no longer afraid of the coach.

Here's how emotions
get from a child to a parent:

Inward Processor → Mind → Parent

Outward Processor → Parent

Inward Processors go through the filter of the mind before you hear what's bothering them. Outward Processors don't have a filter. When it lands in their brain, it lands in your lap. That's why it's important to not overreact to what Outward Processors say. They'll say lots of things they don't mean and exaggerate many of their feelings, because when you talk a lot, a lot of things come out.

How They Deal with Feelings

Inward Processors are good at denying feelings. It's not that they're trying to deny their feelings, it's just that talking about feelings is so difficult. When I do a feelings activity with an Inward Processing child, I have to remember this. After all, I am an Outward Processor and have always loved talking about my feelings. So when I sit down with an Inward Processor, I imagine what it would be like if I walked into a therapist's office and she said, "You can only use one hundred words to describe your situation. Think carefully about what you want to say." I would panic, because I know I need more like one thousand words to process what I am experiencing.

On the other hand, the Inward Processor sitting in front of me is panicking because I am giving him one-thousand-plus words, and he can't imagine what to say. In this case, I make things simple. I ask him to choose a feeling card and tell me why he feels that way. Essentially, all he has to do is choose a card and say, "I feel _____ because _____." This is a far better scenario than me saying, "How are you feeling about your parents' divorce?" That question is too scary and open-ended for an Inward Processor to handle.

Inward Processors tend to minimize feelings or talk about them only after they've passed. After the piano recital is over, they'll say, "I was nervous," or after the basketball championship, they'll say, "I couldn't sleep last night." All the while, you thought they were fine. Or rather, you may not have thought they were fine. You may have been noticing their behavior all along and even asked them about it, but they denied anything was wrong. Even if they do share their feelings, they will generally minimize them to the point where you never really knew how bad they were.

Outward Processors exaggerate feelings. They tell you how bad their life is, how bad you are making them feel, and how hard things are for them. "You don't know what it's like!" is a typical response from an Outward Processor, and the truth is, you may not. You may not know how it feels to be that anxious or unable to take your mind off something. But leave it to an Outward Processor to remind you.

When this occurs, it's hard not to try to bring the Outward Processor down to a more rational place. "It's not that bad," is what many parents say to their Outward Processor. This may be the truth, but an Outward Processor will never agree. To them, feelings are huge, and arguing with them only leads to more frustration.

How They Handle Blame

Inward Processors are good at blaming others. They hate to be wrong, rarely admit to making mistakes, and will often blame siblings for their problems. Siblings are the target of choice for Inward Processors because siblings are the safest target and because siblings push their buttons the most. Blaming siblings is a lot easier than blaming parents (where they risk getting in trouble) or friends (where they risk losing social status). There is very little to lose when blaming siblings, and Inward Processors know it.

Inward Processors blame others because they don't know why they're upset. Their thoughts are all jumbled up in their brain and they can't make sense of them. Kids want to feel better just as much as you want them to feel better, but Inward Processors aren't sure just how to do it. By making someone else out to be the bad guy, they deflect the problem away from themselves and begin to feel some relief.

On the other hand, Outward Processors tend to place blame on themselves. They say things like: "I can't do it!" "It's too hard." "I'm too scared." "I'll never be able to handle it." Outward Processors doubt themselves, don't think they can handle situations, and make themselves out to be more incapable than they really are. Outward Processors are glass half-empty thinkers. Things will never get better, they'll never feel better, and life is always going to be a struggle.

Several of the tools, including "I Did It!" List (Tool #5) and The Marble System (Tool #6) can help change this dynamic with Outward Processors. The tools help them see themselves in an empowered, positive light, and any time an Outward Processor can feel empowered, it is a good day.

How to Help Kids Process Emotions

Now that we know how Inward and Outward Processors think and act, it's important to know what parents can do to help. Specifically, how to help Inward Processors communicate and how to help Outward Processors solve problems on their own. Let's start with how to help Inward Processors communicate.

How to Help Inward Processors Communicate

First of all, this is not easy. If you've tried getting to the root of your Inward Processor's behavior without much success, you're not alone. Inward Processors can and will open up, but it might not be in the typical way. The way most parents try to get their kids to open up is by asking them questions. If you're doing this as a parent, stop. Asking a child more questions after they've refused to answer is like giving your child the key to your own jail cell. You are giving away your power and laying it in the lap of your child. Silence is power, especially when a child is angry. They will refuse to answer questions as a way to retain their power.

What does help Inward Processors to open up is taking the focus off of them. This occurs when you change the direction of the conversation or tell a story that is applicable.

You change the direction of the conversation by no longer engaging in the current conversation. Changing the Channel (Tool #3) is a great example of this. In changing the direction of the conversation, if you appear like you don't care, you will further enrage your child. However, if you tactfully move on to something else, kids will often move on as well. Then, after you've moved on, come back and address the situation. This allows Inward Processors time to calm down and sort out their thoughts. Changing the direction of the conversation looks like this:

Child: I'm not going to the recital!

Parent: I heard you.

Child: I'm not going!

Parent: I heard you, but I'd rather talk about what we're going to do afterward.

Child: What? What are we going to do afterward?

Parent: Remember that ice cream place across town?

Child: Yes. Are we going? Really?

Parent: After the recital, yes, we are going to get ice cream.

Telling children stories also works great with Inward Processors. Stories take the focus off the child and place it on someone else. You could find stories in books or make them up yourself. Either way, Inward Processors will open up when they feel they connected with the person in the story.

When I am in session with an Inward Processor, I will often tell a story about another child I work with who has a similar issue. Suddenly, the Inward Processor wants to talk about the issue, specifically, how to help the other child feel better, and their ideas are great! I couldn't have picked better solutions myself. As you might suspect, while the child is so busy helping the other kid out, he's opening up about his own experience and giving me a window into his anxiety.

Here's an example: "I work with this kid who's really anxious. Every time he comes in he tells me how afraid he is of the monsters underneath his bed. Every night he thinks those monsters are going to reach out and grab his ankles. I'm trying to come up with ideas for him but am not sure what will work."

The child I'm working with is suddenly hooked. Because he's also afraid of monsters, he immediately identifies with the other child and wants to help him. Either he will admit he's afraid of monsters too, or he will give me a number of suggestions to help the other child. He will offer suggestions such as: "Tell him to keep a night-light on," or "Tell him that monsters aren't real." When he says this, I will say, "That's a great idea. Do you think that will work for you?" to help him connect the dots.

By using The Worry Expert (Tool #14), you can help your child in the same way by telling him stories of things you were afraid of in your own childhood or by choosing books from the library that target the same fears your child has. Even if the books don't give concrete examples of how the child conquers the fears, the power of both the books and personal stories are that they normalize feelings. Once kids understand that other kids face the same problems, they don't feel so alone and become more motivated to try and overcome their fears.

How to Help Outward Processors Learn Boundaries

If your child is an Outward Processor, he's going to need to learn boundaries. Boundaries help Outward Processors learn how to self-soothe, and by self-soothing, they can begin solving their problems. Worry Time (Tool #2) and The Five Question Rule (Tool #4) in Part Two are designed to help children do just that. Having hour-long conversations about your child's worries is not only bad for you, it's bad for your child.

Setting boundaries means not allowing your child to talk incessantly about his worries. There's a time and a place for talking about fears, but when you're holding a pot of boiling water, driving through heavy traffic, or fixing lunches, you shouldn't be expected to solve your child's worries.

Boundaries not only help kids become more patient in their conversations with you, but also in conversations with peers. Kids who adhere to their parents' boundaries will be more adaptable to conversations and will learn to process their fears without coming to you all the time. Kids who can process emotions on their own feel more empowered than kids who need you to make them feel better.

Making the Most of Communication

Whether you're dealing with an Inward Processor or an Outward Processor, it's important to make the most of those times you have to talk. In a time of cell phones and text messages, kids suffer from a lack of undivided attention that used to exist before technology became such a part of our daily lives. When parents come to me looking for better ways to communicate, I encourage them to turn their cell phones on silent while they're in the car with their kids. Car rides can be a great time to talk to your kids and a terrible time to talk to friends. Kids get extremely jealous when you pick them up from school with a phone to your ear. From their perspective, you've had all day to talk to your friends, and now it's time for them. So turn your cell phone on silent and check Facebook while they're at school.

It's also important to make time for one-on-one interactions. Inward Processors will often open up on a hike far from home or while sharing an ice cream on a Saturday afternoon. They need the time and space to begin talking, and during one-on-one time with you, they have it. Outward Processors need the same time. Even though they will talk more openly about feelings during the course of a day, they still need those moments of having your full attention. Having individual time with parents gives kids the opportunity to share what's really going on with them.

4

How to Address Your Child's Anxiety in an Age of Worry

. . . .

We are currently in the age of anxiety. Anxiety has never been more prevalent, has never received as much attention, and has never had as many treatment options as it does in our current times. Famous stars share their struggles with anxiety, antianxiety medications fill television commercials, and the number of anxiety books, toolkits, iPhone apps, and ebooks available are enough to make our heads spin.

Why is anxiety so prevalent? Some researchers blame the stress-filled society we live in, while others blame genetics, technology, and the media. Still, no one can answer why there are currently 7.8 million anxious kids in the United States (National Institute of Mental Health). Even if we did know the answer, it seems we're stuck with the world we live in. We can't seem to live in our world, yet we can't seem to remove ourselves from it. The amount of information we have in front of us is just too tempting.

There are both pros and cons of parenting an anxious child in the world in which we live versus ten, twenty, or thirty years ago.

The pros: There are more resources than ever before. With the click of a button, you can have access to thousands of articles about anxiety. In five minutes, you can join a parent support group with people from all over the world. You can research medications, doctors, and the various treatments for anxiety, and by the time you actually sit down with a therapist, you can diagnose your child with anxiety simply because you've taken an online test and he's met every criteria. Today's parents are more informed than ever before.

The cons: No matter how hard you try to protect your child, today's kids are subjected to huge amounts of information—information they have no business knowing. Even if you aren't letting your child watch CNN, some of his classmates' parents are. Even though you didn't tell your child about the break-in down the street, another parent did, and the child of that parent passed the information along to your child at recess. Unless you homeschool your child and he isn't allowed to play independently with other kids, your child will be exposed to the very information you've worked so hard to keep from him.

How to Address Your Child's Anxiety

Not every child who is anxious needs to see a therapist. Nor does every child need to see a psychiatrist or go on medication. As a parent, there are steps you can take before seeking outside help, and one of those steps may very well be reading this book. After all, some kids simply need parents to help them learn how to handle their anxiety. Given the right information and tools, many parents see their child's anxiety dramatically decrease.

If, after reading the book and implementing the tools, you still need help with your child's anxiety, you may want to seek out a child psychotherapist to give you extra support, as well as to work with your child individually. In this chapter we're going to look at the kinds of options that are out there.

One Therapist Does Not Fit All

Finding a psychotherapist who treats anxiety is not difficult. Anxiety is the number-one reason people seek out therapy, making anxiety the most treated mental health disorder in the United States. In fact, people with anxiety disorders are three to five times more likely to go to the doctor than those who do not suffer from anxiety.

Finding a therapist who treats anxiety is simple; finding one who treats anxiety *and* works with children is not (we'll discuss this more later in the chapter). Because of the growing number of childhood-anxiety referrals, there is a growing need for therapists who specialize in working with children.

Psychotherapy originated as talk therapy and has maintained an emphasis on "talking" out problems. While this method works great for adults, it doesn't work so well for kids. Even so, the majority of graduate psychology programs remain focused on training their students in talk therapy. If you want to work with kids, you have to get specialized training in child development, set up your office differently than those who work with adults, and be well versed in child development.

How Kids' Brains Are Different from Adults' Brains

Child psychotherapists have an understanding of how kids' brains work. They don't expect a child to come in and "talk" about issues when they aren't developmentally at the stage where talking is most appropriate. When we expect children to communicate just with words, we are expecting them to act like "little adults," something which is asked of them too much of the time. Children don't have the cognitive ability to think like adults do. So, even if I tried, I could not get an eight-year-old to adopt my perspective on his anxiety. Our brains are completely different. To better understand how kids' brains work, let's look at *Piaget's stages of cognitive development*.

Piaget's Stages of Cognitive Development:

1. **Sensorimotor: 0–2.** Children use motor activity instead of symbols. Knowledge is based on physical interactions and experiences, therefore is limited.
2. **Preoperational: 2–7.** Children enjoy make-believe and can understand the difference between the past and the future. Complex concepts, such as cause-and-effect relationships, have not been learned.
3. **Concrete operational: 7–11.** Children can manipulate symbols that are related to concrete objects. Thinking becomes less egocentric with increased awareness of external events, and involves concrete references.
4. **Formal operational: 11–lifespan.** Adolescents and adults can understand abstract concepts. They can think about multiple variables in systematic ways, can formulate hypotheses, and think about abstract relationships and concepts.

Child psychotherapists take these stages into account and bring the therapy to the level of the child. For example, if a child is

developmentally eight years old, they would do activities at his current level—the concrete operational stage of development. Piaget's
stages of development suggest children are able to grasp concepts
only in the stage in which they are currently functioning. So for
an eight-year-old, we would use concrete objects to work on
abstract issues.

For example, if a child is worried about monsters, we make
monsters out of clay and pummel them. Then we draw monsters
on paper and rip them up. We make wristbands that will protect
us from monsters and make a Monster-Free Zone sign to hang up
above the bed. These are all concrete techniques that help kids with
abstract issues. After all, what is a monster? Nothing more than an
image a child has created in his mind. And because the mind is good
at distorting things, doing concrete activities gets the fear out of a
child's mind and onto something he can control. Once it's out of his
mind and in front of him, he can pummel it, rip it up, and ultimately
feel less afraid.

Therapy Options

Therapy can be a great way for kids to learn how to manage their
anxiety. In therapy, kids can learn anxiety-reduction techniques as
well as have a safe place to share their fears. The therapy process can
last as little as six weeks or as long as a year, depending on what types
of issues the child is bringing in. For example, if it is just anxiety a
child is struggling with, anxiety-reduction tools can be implemented,
and a child can get better rather quickly. If a child is also struggling
with low self-esteem, anger management, and impulse control, the
process can take much longer.

The best way to find a therapist is to ask for a recommendation from your child's school counselor, pediatrician, or from other parents. School counselors and pediatricians are in the role of making outside referrals and are usually aware of the best professionals in the community. Other parents are also a great resource, especially if they have a child who has been through the therapy process. They can tell you what to expect, how the process works, and how their child benefitted from the sessions.

There is always a consideration of cost when it comes to therapy, and depending on the area in which you live and what type of professional you are seeking out, the cost will vary. Some therapists charge as little as $60 a session, and some charge nearly $200. If you have an insurance policy that covers mental-health services, you may also use your insurance, but be aware that anytime you use your insurance, there will be a mental-health diagnosis assigned to your child. The diagnosis will stay on your child's mental-health record indefinitely, so make sure you are okay with that before you file anything with your insurance company.

In deciding on a therapist, be aware that there are a lot of options out there. There are child psychologists who still use talk therapy as their primary mode of communication, and there are therapists who work with mostly adults but are willing to see kids too. Then, there are therapists who specialize in treating kids, and for the purpose of this book, we will look at those more in detail, the first of which are Play Therapists.

Play Therapy

Play Therapy is the therapy of choice in working with children ages three through twelve. Play Therapy is built on the belief that play is the language of children, and toys are their words. Children communicate best when they are able to play out their issues instead of merely talking about them.

There are two main types of Play Therapy: Non-Directive Play Therapy and Directive Play Therapy, and many therapists (like me) often use both approaches within the same session. During Non-Directive Play Therapy, the child is allowed to choose the toys and the materials (such as sand, clay, markers, etc.) and manipulate them however he chooses. During Non-Directive Play Therapy, the therapist "tracks" the play by making statements such as "The dinosaur is angry just like you get angry" to help the child understand his own relationship to his world.

During Directive Play Therapy, the therapist chooses the toys and/or activities that target the child's specific needs. For example, in working with an anxious child, the therapist would say, "I'm going to teach you a technique to help you calm down when you're feeling worried," and encourage the child to use the technique outside of the session. When working with anxious kids, I generally begin with directive techniques, such as anxiety-reduction tools, and spend the last fifteen to twenty minutes in Non-Directive Play Therapy, allowing a child to do whatever he chooses. Often times, kids will reveal thoughts and feelings during Non-Directive Play Therapy that they wouldn't share otherwise. That's because playing creates a comfortable environment where kids can share thoughts and feelings on their level rather than on an adult level.

When you walk into the office of a Play Therapist, you will see a variety of materials you won't see in a traditional therapist's office. You might see a tray of Moon Sand, a puppet tree, shelves of miniatures, clay, PlayDoh, Model Magic, markers, therapeutic games, and so on. Many adult therapists will also see teenagers but often shy away from anyone under twelve, because working with young children without age-appropriate toys is difficult. Kids often get restless, feel uncomfortable, and end up trying to talk like an adult about their problems without much success.

Play has been recognized as important since the time of Plato (429–347 BC) who reportedly observed, "You can discover more about a person in an hour of play than in a year of conversation." Currently, there is an Association for Play Therapy (www.a4pt.org), an *International Journal of Play Therapy*, a Play Therapy magazine, and thousands of Play Therapists around the world. There is also a Registered Play Therapist designation, which includes two thousand hours of clinical supervision in Play Therapy, along with 150 hours of specific Play Therapy training. This, in addition to a graduate degree, psychology training, and maintaining a mental-health license, keeps many clinicians from becoming Registered Play Therapists. If you are looking for a therapist for your child, ask about their experience with Play Therapy. Also, educate yourself about Play Therapy and how it can benefit your child.

The Acceptance Model and Mindfulness

There are many ways to treat anxiety, and the way in which a therapist was trained is often the model they stick with. The older generation of therapists was trained to treat issues from a cognitive perspective and use techniques such as Cognitive-Behavioral Therapy (CBT) to treat anxious children. CBT is widely researched and has shown impressive results. CBT essentially encourages children to either replace or eliminate negative thoughts. The idea behind this is that if kids can change the way they think about their fears, they will become less anxious.

The younger generation of psychotherapists is trained to treat issues from an acceptance perspective. Instead of trying to get rid of fears, we are now teaching kids to accept and work with them. For example, instead of trying to get rid of the thought: *I can't go outside. I'm too scared*, therapists are now helping kids acknowledge the thought and learn to relax within it. Relaxation techniques are now being taught to kids, not only in therapy offices but in schools around the country.

Books such as *The Mindful Child* by Susan Kaiser Greenland are helping teachers, parents, and child-care workers learn how to help kids become more aware of themselves and less reactive to their outside world. Activities such as breathing with a puppet on your belly and taking five minutes to eat a raisin are some of the techniques that are helping kids learn to slow down. Mindfulness isn't new; it has been used in adult psychotherapy for a number of years, but it's finally seeping into our work with kids.

In my own practice, I help kids identify where they feel worry in their body and learn to give it a name. By using tools such as Naming the Anxiety (Tool #11), I help kids learn not to identify with their anxiety by giving it a name such as "Worry Walter." We talk about how it feels when "Worry Walter" comes to visit, how their body changes, how their mind starts going fast, and then how it feels when he leaves: their shoulders relax, their stomach stops hurting, they begin to laugh. With this technique, I help kids become more aware of how they're feeling, both when they're anxious and when they're not. After all, anxiety comes in waves, and learning how to ride it out is one of the most effective tools an anxious child can have.

In my work with kids, I include cognitive strategies as well as acceptance and mindfulness. After all, different kids respond to different things. Some kids respond well to changing negative thoughts, and some respond better to breathing and awareness techniques. In my experience, teaching anxious kids a variety of tools from different perspectives provides the best results. Kids can then choose what works best for them.

Medication

One of the first thing parents of anxious kids ask me is, "Does my child have to go on medication?" Putting a child on medication is a huge decision, and not one to take lightly. Medication can improve the overall mood and behavior in children, making their lives at both home and school much easier. Parents also report major improvements in their child's ability to respond appropriately to instructions and that the overall tone in the home can improve once a child is on medication. Even so, many parents are often leery of putting their children on medication. When I meet with parents, I encourage them to try therapy first, especially in dealing with anxiety issues. If, after three months, your child is still struggling with anxiety, I encourage parents to use the "2 out of 3 Rule."

The 2 Out of 3 Rule

My general rule of thumb when it comes to medication is that if your child is suffering in two out of the three main areas of life, it is time to look at medication. The three main areas are:

1. **School**—This includes academics and behavior. If your child is unable to learn, focus, or participate in class, then you can count school as an area of weakness.

2. **Home**—The home environment includes the ability to follow rules, be respectful to parents and siblings, and maintain a level of self-control.

3. **Friends**—This includes the ability to maintain friendships, to attend social functions, behave appropriately in social settings, to initiate play with friends, and to be comfortable in social situations.

If all three areas are suffering, it's often too much for kids to handle. Kids need something to boost their confidence, to empower them, and to make them feel better. When that something isn't there, things begin to snowball. If kids aren't doing well at home and at school, they get no relief. If they've lost friends as well, then they'll feel completely overwhelmed. When these situations occur, medication can be helpful to get the ball rolling in a positive direction. A psychiatrist friend of mine says that medications help turn the volume down. By that he means when a child is feeling enormous amounts of anxiety, his mental volume is about a ten. Medication can bring it down to a five, a level in which he can think more rationally and get some relief.

Even if only one of the three areas is affected, pay special attention if it's school. The school setting has both academic and social consequences, so the stakes are higher. If a child misses class or work and loses friends, there will be two areas affected rather than just one. Especially for kids who are refusing to go to school, medication can be a faster way to getting them back into the classroom. It's also important to have the school involved in helping your child be successful. In the end, support from teachers and the administration makes all the difference when anxiety is showing up at school.

Putting the Pieces Together

Once you know your child is anxious, you can begin putting the pieces of the puzzle together. Reading books, talking with teachers, school counselors, testing professionals, and even contacting a therapist: all of these are pieces you may want to use. Here are some guidelines for how you can head in the right direction.

Coordinating with the School

If your child's anxiety is coming out at school, make sure to let the teacher know you are addressing the issue at home. The placebo effect really works here! I continually meet with parents who say, "Things have gotten better since I called you." Why is that? Because the relief of getting help makes people see the situation as already improved. This goes the same for teachers. If a teacher knows you are working on things at home, the situation in her eyes is already improved, which will probably make your child's day go much easier.

It is also important to get feedback from your child's teacher about how things are going at school. This can come in the form of a daily note in your child's folder, through weekly emails, or by having periodic parent/teacher meetings. This will give you a better understanding of what your child is being triggered by and how you can help him at home. For example, if your child is becoming anxious before tests, you can remind him to do Square Breathing

(Tool #1) before the test begins. If he is anxious around peers, you can set up additional play dates on weekends to help him develop closer relationships with the kids in his class.

School counselors are also great resources for anxious children. While school counselors don't do therapy, they are able to work with children individually and in groups to help them become more comfortable at school. School counselors are often called on by the teacher to talk to a student who seems upset or overly anxious during the school day. Kids who are having problems with friends or difficulties being away from their parents may also find themselves in the school counselor's office. I spent eight years as a school counselor and found that during the course of a school day, kids can become upset and need someone to talk to. Since teachers are busy teaching the other students in class, school counselors can give kids the one-on-one time they need. They are also more aware of the social and emotional issues of students and are trained to know how to handle difficult situations teachers do not have the time to deal with.

Psychological Testing

School psychologists are also a great resource to children in the school setting. School psychologists have received specific training, and in addition to the master's degree school counselors must obtain, they must receive an educational specialist degree that enables them to gain a greater understanding of the learning and emotional difficulties children face. School psychologists consult with administrators, teachers, and school counselors and, when it is appropriate, conduct psychological testing within the school setting. School psychologists conduct not only testing for learning disabilities but also for giftedness. Because of this, many smart kids have been evaluated by a school psychologist at one point or another.

If your child is not in the public-school setting, you may need to find an outside evaluator to conduct psychological testing. There are several advantages to having an outside evaluator test your child, including a faster turnaround time (in most cases) and the ability to choose whether you share the test with the school. It can be beneficial to share the results with your child's teacher, as it will help the teacher understand your child better, but some parents choose to keep the test to themselves. Regardless, psychological testing can identify issues parents might not otherwise pick up on.

Using objective tests, such as the Rorschach Inkblot Test and the Thematic Apperception Test, psychological testing measures how your child feels about himself, along with his relationship to parents, siblings, and the family as a whole. Using pictures, incomplete sentences, inkblots, and so forth, psychological testing opens the window into your child's world.

Especially if a child isn't good at expressing feelings, having testing conducted with a psychologist who specializes in testing children will help uncover what is really going on with your child. Does he feel excluded now that he has a younger sibling? Does he see himself as competent? Does he feel connected to his peers? Is he happy? These are the answers you'll receive in the final results. As a general rule, the psychologists who do the testing are not the psychologists who will actually be helping your child with his anxiety. You will need to go to someone who specializes in testing, and then share the results with your child's therapist.

Finding the Right Therapist

Every therapist has a different way of working with kids. Depending on training, experience, and overall personality, therapists vary widely in how they treat kids and how they work with the family as a whole. The best way to determine if a therapist is right for your child is to meet prior to your child meeting with him. This allows you to share background information and learn about the therapist's approach, along with getting an overall sense of whether your child will be able to connect to the therapist.

After meeting with the therapist, I would recommend you spend at least three sessions determining whether the therapist is a good fit. After your child walks out of the first session, you may know immediately it is a good fit by your child's sense of relief and positive things to say about the session. If your child walks out without such enthusiasm, give it another two sessions to see if things change. If after three sessions your child doesn't seem like he's made a connection, let the therapist know, and either he can change the structure of the sessions, or you can find a new therapist. Overall, it's important for kids to have a good experience so they don't feel punished for having anxiety. Instead, they will feel happy they have someone to talk to about it.

Talking to Your Child about Therapy

If you are going to take your child to therapy, it's important to frame it in the right way. Anxious kids are going to be concerned about meeting someone new and talking about things they would normally only tell their parents. Without an idea of what to expect, they can worry about the appointment for weeks ahead of time. My general rule of thumb is this: tell your child the day before the appointment, not any sooner. If you tell your child three weeks before, he'll worry for three weeks. The exception to this rule is if your child is excited about going to therapy, because then telling him will give him some relief.

Secondly, use positive and fun language. Instead of saying, "We are going to have to figure out your anxiety. I'm taking you to talk to someone," say, "I met this really nice lady who talks to kids about their feelings. She has lots of cool toys and works with a lot of kids your age." Toys are the key here. Just like I mentioned in the Play Therapy section, toys make kids feel at ease. Having toys in your office lets kids know you want them to be comfortable.

Setting Goals

Setting reasonable goals for your anxious child is important. If your child has Generalized Anxiety, expecting the anxiety to go away for good is simply not reasonable. After all, the genetic make-up of many kids makes them prone to anxiety

Instead, a reasonable goal for any anxious child is to take action despite fear. Even though they're scared, they'll still go into the classroom. Even though they're afraid of shots, they'll still walk into the doctor's office, and even though they miss you terribly, they'll still go sleepaway camp. They learn to face their fears and overcome them. Instead of running away they say, "I'm afraid but I'm still going."

When they overcome their fears, kids get a huge boost of confidence. Instead of believing they can't do something, they believe they can. They feel empowered, and an empowered child can do just about anything. The only way for anxious kids to get this empowerment is to face their fears and come out on the other side. Every anxiety-producing event your child overcomes will increase his confidence level. Every anxiety-producing event your child avoids will decrease his confidence level.

A child who faces his fear becomes confident. Confident children might still feel afraid at times, but their fear does not keep them from taking action. They are able to do the things they want, attend the activities everyone else is attending, and are still able sleep at night.

The Final Puzzle Pieces

Some parents find a therapist, have a good evaluation conducted, coordinate with the school, *and* have their child put on medication, and other parents do only one or two of the above. Regardless of how you choose to proceed, childhood anxiety can and will get better if your child has the proper support. If you are going to choose only one thing to do, however, I would start by using the tools listed in the second part of this book. Secondly, I would have a therapist teach your child anxiety-management tools. Tools allow kids to feel empowered enough to manage what happens in their lives. If things don't improve, I would look at testing and then medication. If you are unsure about what your child needs, you can consult with a child psychotherapist to discuss what your child might benefit from most.

5

Where Intelligence and Anxiety Collide

• •

S ome parents of smart kids notice their children are more emotional than other kids. They notice them having a hard time
transitioning. They can't understand why they won't sleep in their
own bed, why they cling to parents and are afraid of things other kids
aren't afraid of. Maybe their child is in the top at school, but he can't
handle the pressure. Maybe he doesn't like homework, complains
about not having friends, won't get out of the car, takes hours to do
homework, and raises concerns for his teacher.

Sometimes the experience of having a smart child isn't what most
parents think it's going to be. In fact, gifted children are twice as
likely to have social and emotional problems as the general popula-
tion of children. Since there are currently three million gifted kids in
the United States, there are a lot of parents out there who are worried, concerned, and confused. They have done everything to help
their child on an intellectual level, but they can't figure out what is
happening emotionally. The answers to these concerns can be found
in the simplest of places—in their child's development.

Asynchronous Development

Asychronous development is a new term for most parents. It isn't talked about among parents and is rarely brought up at school. All the while, it is having compounding effects on smart kids around the country. So what is asynchronous development?

Asynchronous development is where intelligence and anxiety collide. It is the place where being smart isn't so advantageous; in fact, it is a liability.

Let's take a six-year-old, for example. A six-year-old should *look*, *think*, and *feel* like a six-year-old.

An average six-year-old's development looks like this:

Physical Development—6

Intellectual Ability—6

Emotional Maturity—6

If you see this six-year-old in a classroom, he will be about the same height as his peers, able to write his name legibly, do simple math, sit at his seat without disturbing others, and initiate play with his peers. This six-year-old will go through school without much of a problem. The work will be challenging, but he'll be able to complete it. If he loses a friend, he'll have the social skills to make new ones. He'll sit in his seat and respond easily to redirection. This six-year-old is what teachers were trained to teach.

However, if a six-year-old experiences a discrepancy in his development, or develops asynchronously, there will be challenges. If he's shorter than his peers, he may feel insecure about his height. If he's emotionally nine years old, he may not be able to understand the social dynamic of the classroom. And, if he thinks like a ten-year-old, he'll be able to understand intellectual concepts he's not ready to deal with emotionally. Below are two common scenarios of children with asynchronous development:

Child #1:

Physical Development—6

Intellectual Ability—9

Emotional Maturity—6

This six-year-old is very different from the first six-year-old. He is still the same size as his peers, but instead of writing his name legibly and doing simple math, he's reading the fifth Harry Potter book. He's able to understand that death can happen to anyone and that tornadoes occur when cold and warm air masses collide. **The good news:** He still has the emotional maturity of other six-year-olds, so the discrepancy between his intellect and emotions is only three years. **The bad news:** what he is able to process intellectually is three years beyond what a six-year-old can handle emotionally.

Child #2:

Physical Development—6

Intellectual Ability—9

Emotional Maturity—4

Child #2 looks like a six-year-old and thinks like a nine-year-old, but acts like a four-year-old. Where Child #1 was only advanced intellectually, Child #2 is both advanced intellectually and delayed emotionally. Instead of a three-year gap between his intellect and emotions, he has a five-year gap. So, even though Child #2 gets 95 percent of the questions right on a statewide achievement test, he can't tell you why he's angry. While he can do multistep division, he throws a tantrum in the Whole Foods parking lot because you won't buy him his choice of snack. He hits his sister, kicks his brother, and claims he can't understand why he gets put in time out. He's afraid of monsters, curls up in a ball when the sky turns gray, and is too anxious to go to the first soccer practice.

A gap like this wreaks havoc on a child's emotional state. He can't understand why other kids don't like him, why Mom spends more time with little brother, and how to get the attention he so desperately needs. Essentially, he can understand advanced topics but can't understand himself.

If you expose him to topics at or above his intellectual level, the discrepancy between his intellect and emotions will become even greater. For example, if he listens to NPR on the way to school and hears about terrorists, he'll be able to understand that terrorists often attack innocent people who work in buildings. He'll be able to take the idea to the next level by understanding that his mom is an innocent person who also works in a building. Here's how he'll process, from his developmental level, what he just heard.

His nine-year-old intellect understands this: *My mother works in a building where a lot of people work. She could get bombed at work today.*

His four-year-old emotional level is capable of this: *I need my mother. I can't live without my mother. I will die without my mother.*

This discrepancy between "my mother could die today" and "if she dies, I die too" is what many children with asynchronous development are dealing with. Their minds go from wondering whom they're going to play with at recess to worrying about whether their mother will die. It's the discrepancy in this scenario that matters, not the terrorists. If a sixteen-year-old hears about terrorists, he can discuss them in his World History class, but a six-year-old is left to deal with it all by himself—such things aren't discussed between finger-painting and addition. After all, a typical six-year-old can't grasp the concept of war. But a smart six-year-old is able to understand that war kills people and that it could also kill him and his family.

Discrepancies

When it comes to development, discrepancies are a big deal. The education system uses the discrepancy between IQ and how a child performs in the classroom to determine whether a child has a learning disability and the discrepancy between an average IQ and a high IQ to determine whether a child is certified gifted. Discrepancies basically tell us that kids need extra support.

For example, when a child has a learning disability in math, schools give him remedial math instruction to help him catch up. When he acquires the skills to do grade-level math, he can begin doing regular classroom work. When children are certified gifted, schools allow them to receive instruction on their advanced level, which heightens their IQ even further. However, instead of determining where kids are on both an intellectual and emotional level, and dealing with any discrepancies, educators focus only on intelligence. And for many gifted kids, the discrepancy between intelligence and emotions doesn't decrease after they become certified gifted, but actually increases.

Here's why. While their minds are growing exponentially, their emotional lives are being all but ignored. They aren't learning how to identify their emotions; they're learning how to identify the next step in a math equation. They aren't learning how they feel about natural disasters; they are learning how tsunamis are formed and how many people were killed in Indonesia. Essentially, we are doing a great job of making kids smarter; but we're failing at making them more self-aware.

The Anxiety Surge

When children experience a discrepancy between intellectual and emotional development, they will often feel a surge of anxiety. It's not that smart kids constantly feel afraid; it's that when their minds get stuck on a fear, they can't focus on anything else.

Let's take Mark, for example. Mark is an eight-year-old boy, and his development looks like this:

Physical Development—8

Intellectual Ability—11

Emotional Maturity—5

Mark is sitting in a third-grade classroom, where he watches a movie about a boy whose parents don't have enough money to pay for college. Mark, who is intellectually eleven, realizes he will be going to college in ten years and isn't sure if his parents will have enough money to send him. His five-year-old emotional state doesn't know how to deal with the reality of not going to college. Suddenly, Mark goes into a panic.

His mind starts jumping to: *What if I can't go to college? How will I make money? What if I don't have enough money to buy food? How am I going to take care of my kids?* These thoughts are running through the mind of a third-grader who still has to do his reading assignment, take a timed math test, work in small groups, and wait for you in the pick-up line.

When you finally pick up Mark, he's had six hours of worry stuck in his brain. Either he will tell you about it, or he won't (as we discussed in Chapter 3), but regardless, he is feeling a surge of thoughts that are causing a tidal wave of emotions he doesn't know how to handle.

Another example is Claire, an eleven-year-old girl whose development looks like this:

Physical Development—11

Intellectual Ability—15

Emotional Maturity—9

Claire goes to a sleepover, where another child shares that her grandmother has cancer. Claire, knowing this girl's grandmother may die, not only feels sad for the girl but can't sleep because she's thinking about her own grandmother. Claire tries to recall the last time she saw her grandmother and becomes panicked by the thought that she might not see her again. Meanwhile, it's 1:00 in the morning, and she's stuck at a sleepover without anyone to talk to about it.

Managing the Surge

If you've never felt a surge of anxiety, you might be surprised by how strong it can be. I was an anxious kid myself and felt my first surge of anxiety when I was four years old and overheard my cousin talking about how women get these "huge shots" when they have babies. I was nervous about my kindergarten shots anyway, but overhearing that conversation took me to a place I had never been before. I now know that feeling as fear and that experience as anxiety. As my mother recalls, I was distant for days. I was withdrawn, didn't want to talk, and, despite her efforts to help, couldn't put into words what I was feeling. That was until the surge came.

The surge came in the middle of the night, when I woke out of a dead sleep with a fear of having a baby. I ran to my mother's room and finally told her what I was afraid of. My mother recalls being baffled by how a four-year-old could be worried about such an advanced topic. As the years went by, however, she came to understand that I was the kind of kid who worried about future things. I worried about things that were years away, things that only adults worried about, things over which I had very little control.

For other kids, the surge happens after seeing a scary movie or reading a scary book. It can happen after a natural disaster or hearing a story where someone dies. The surge happens in a variety of ways, but once it occurs, childhood seems completely different. For me, it opened a can of worms I couldn't figure out how to close. Suddenly, I became afraid of everything. I worried about the end of the world, paying for college, growing old, making money, and having a career. And even though I tried, I couldn't find much of anything to make it go away.

As adults, we know what to do when we're anxious. We take a bath, go for a run, call a friend, or read something inspirational. The point is we recognize that we're anxious, and we do something about it. To recognize you're feeling a certain way requires the ability to be objective, and the ability to be objective lies in two parts of the brain:

1. **Corpus callosum**—a fiber system that relays information between the two hemispheres of the brain
2. **Prefrontal cortex**—the CEO of the brain, responsible for planning, working memory, organization, and modulating mood

Both the corpus callosum and the prefrontal cortex are responsible for higher level functioning, and both are not fully developed until the early twenties. (This is largely the reason adolescents behave so erratically.)

This is also why kids get so stuck in anxiety. Their brains are not developed enough to become objective. Objectivity is the ability to realize you're anxious about something that either (1) won't happen, or (2) you can do very little about. In Claire's case, her grandmother probably didn't develop cancer while she was at the sleepover, nor does Mark have to worry about paying for college seven years ahead of time. However, with underdeveloped brains, children aren't able to see this on their own.

Bridging the Gap

Because intellectual development will be focused on at school, it's important to focus on emotional development at home. For kids, childhood is all about learning. Instead of your child's anxiety coming out at the workplace someday, it's best for him to learn how to deal with it while he's still under your roof.

As your child gets older, long talks will replace feelings cards, and weekend trips will replace car rides to and from school. However, the goal is still the same. Having a connection with your child is far more important than merely having your child follow your rules. If he can connect with you, he'll be better able to express himself with his college roommate, his coworker, and later on, his spouse. Once a person learns how to communicate emotions effectively, life gets a lot easier.

The goal is that at some point, your child's emotions will catch up to his intelligence. He will be able to express his emotions as well as he can solve a math problem. For some people, this never happens. They are very smart but socially and/or emotionally awkward.

However, for the kids who have early intervention around emotional development, they can learn how to be not only smart, but also well-rounded and socially functional.

Holding Objectivity for Your Child

As a parent, you will hold the place of objectivity for your child. Holding objectivity simply means you pay attention to when your child is anxious and begin to see patterns in your child's anxiety. You will notice that he doesn't want to go to school on Mondays, that he fidgets nervously in the car before a soccer game, and that he doesn't have an appetite before his piano recital. As the holder of his objectivity, you can help him become more aware of his own reactions to the outside world.

The first step to holding objectivity for your child is by tracking his anxiety. You can write it down on a small piece of paper, record it in your smartphone, or write it on a calendar. It's simple enough to write a number 1–10, write "high," "medium," or "low," or keep an actual journal. I found tracking anxiety to be such an important part of my work with parents, that I created an iPhone app called *Anxiety Tracker* just for that purpose.

What's important about tracking is that you measure anxiety and give a reason for it. For example, tracking can look like this:

Monday—8, worried about going to school, biting nails, cried on the way to school

Or it could look like this:

Monday—High: School

In the first example, the 8 is a ranking from 1–10, and in the second example, "high" means your child's anxiety was worse than it usually is. Both examples gave "school" as the reason, and remember, it's just as important to track why your child is anxious as it is to track how much anxiety he's experiencing.

The second step is to use the information you tracked to help your child become more aware of his feelings. If you notice your child gets worried every Sunday evening and gets a stomachache, you would say, "Your stomach seems to hurt every Sunday. Are you worried about school?" If your child worries about something that occurs at the same time every year, you can say, "I remember you worrying about that last year." By making your child aware of his patterns, you are essentially helping him become more aware of himself, thus increasing his emotional development.

How to Raise Emotional Intelligence

Because smart kids just get smarter, it's important to find ways to raise your child's Emotional Intelligence so the gap between intelligence and emotions isn't quite so wide. Emotional Intelligence, better known as EQ, has been a hot topic in the last several years, and with all of the bullying incidents, suicides, and school shootings we've seen recently, there has been an influx of resources on how to help children be more emotionally sound.

In speaking about this issue, let's first acknowledge that in the United States we're not very good at expressing emotions. When we have a family member die, we get two days off from work. At most, a week. In a week's time, we'd better have dealt with the grief of losing a parent, a child, or a spouse and be back to working at a high level. This goes the same for our children. When they cry, we shush them. When they scream, we run to the car. We teach our kids to keep their feelings inside until they get home, and then, if we have time, we'll deal with them.

I was on a boat in Peru a few years back when I saw a man and his young son come on board. His son was crying, and his father, in an attempt to soothe him, rubbed his back. After a few minutes of sobbing, the young boy looked up and saw a woman sitting next to him. She had come on board alone and clearly did not know the boy. The boy, who I assume needed the comfort of a woman, simply laid his head on her shoulder. The woman noticed him and, instead of moving away or tapping the father on the shoulder, simply lifted her arm, and the boy fell against her body.

Sitting behind her, I watched the woman rub the crying boy's head as if he were her own. The father, completely trusting of the woman, just looked out on the water as his boy fell asleep. I couldn't take my eyes off what I was seeing. I just kept thinking: *That would never happen in the United States.*

First of all, in the United States, the father would have been trying to hush the boy from the start. Secondly, no woman in her right mind holds a child that isn't hers or that she doesn't have permission to hold for fear of being accused of something. And lastly, for every other person on that boat, hearing a young boy cry is not what we paid for. Thus, in the United States, when kids cry, parents get looks. Those looks make parents panic and search for a way to "fix" their child's emotions. When we try to "fix" children's emotions in public, we send the message that emotions aren't okay to express. While some emotions are not appropriate (such as destroying things or hurting people), crying and being frustrated are just part of childhood. Therefore, kids need to know it's okay to feel what they feel as long as they aren't hurting others in the meantime.

There are several ways to raise emotional intelligence so kids can get to a place where they can feel their emotions and express them appropriately.

Step 1: Connect with your own emotions.

Part of the reason we have trouble understanding our children's emotions is we are disconnected from our own. With the pressures of working, raising children, volunteering at school, and running from scheduled activity to scheduled activity, we hardly have time to know how we feel, let alone how our kids feel.

Therefore, the first step in raising your child's EQ is to be aware of how you are feeling within a given day. Check in with yourself while you're cooking dinner, waiting in the car pool lane, or taking your child to soccer. Notice how your body feels, especially if your child's anxiety is creating anxiety in you. This is something I often discover in working with parents. They say, "I'm so anxious when I pick him up, because I don't know what kind of mood he's going to be in."

The truth is, if you're anxious, you're going to create more anxiety for your child. That's why it's more important to focus on yourself while you're anxious than it is to focus on your child. Just by taking a few deep breaths and relaxing, you can be of more help to your child than if you jump straight to focusing on his feelings.

Step 2: Talk openly about your child's feelings.

An easy way to start a line of communication is to begin a daily routine of connecting around your child's feelings. Trying to juggle two or three kids in the middle of a hectic day does not promote emotional expression. Instead, make a date where you and your child can do something together, just the two of you. You can also set up a specific time each day to do Feelings Check-In (Tool #15) so your child will have an opportunity to share what's been going on in his world. During this time you can ask questions about school, friends, home, and how he feel about each of those areas. You can also share your own feelings about how your child is doing. Saying things like, "I was so excited for you when you got that A" or "I was sad when I learned you didn't get to sit by Sofia" will help your child know you are on his side.

Step 3: Model appropriate emotions.

While parents are not the sole reason for their children's behavior, how they manage their emotions does have an effect on kids. Parents are role models for their child's emotions. Parents teach kids how to control anger, how to react to sadness, and how to openly express feelings.

Parents unknowingly model how to handle emotions every day. They get a call from a distraught friend on the car ride home from school and have to act like nothing is wrong until they get to a place where they can talk privately. Parents deal with money stress, work stress, household chores, and schedule stress, and still make time to hear how their child's day went. The result of this calm handling of emotions, however, is that kids aren't aware their parents are dealing with emotions at all. Parents do a great job of holding it together, and while that can be useful at times, it doesn't allow kids to understand that their parents are people too and that they too sometimes struggle with their feelings.

In my sessions with kids, I normalize feelings by giving examples of the struggles faced by other kids I'm working with. With a focus on maintaining confidentiality, I'll tell them about a child struggling with the exact thing they're struggling with. I'll also tell them about a time I struggled with something as a child, and kids will open up immediately. They'll jump in and tell me about how something similar is happening to them. They beg me to tell them more stories about my childhood and ask to hear them over and over again. Why? Because sharing my emotions makes me real, and many kids don't see adults as real.

I remember the first time I saw my third-grade teacher at the grocery store. I was in disbelief that she went shopping at the same store my family did. In my mind, she was just a teacher. She taught school, lived at school, and did nothing else, but when I saw her at the same store, she became more relatable to me. We now had the grocery store in common, and the next time I saw her, I felt more connected to her. While you don't want to reveal disturbing information that will make your child worry, talking about things you were afraid of as a child and/or friendship issues you experienced will draw a child right in. It takes the focus off of them, and once the pressure is off, they may begin opening up about things they've never shared before.

Step 4: Separate emotions from behaviors.

This is a very important step and where parents often experience the most frustration. While expressing emotions is great for kids, acting out is not. For many anxious kids, a surge of emotion will cause them to act out in strong ways. After all, a symptom of anxiety is irritability, so anxious kids are often highly reactive and highly irritable. This combination causes a vast amount of anxious kids to yell, hit, and otherwise cause great disruption.

When anxious kids act out, it's important to let them know that while it's okay to feel angry, it's not okay to hit. For example, you can say this to your child in times of disruption. "I know you're angry, but hitting is not allowed." When you say this, you are acknowledging your child's feelings but also setting a boundary. You can further support your child by saying, "You can hit a pillow if that helps you feel better, but hitting your sister is not okay." When your child is out of Rational Mind, he will need a target for his frustration. Left to his own devices, he will likely make the wrong choice.

Learning What's Right Takes Time

Learning how to manage their emotions is a skill many anxious people will spend a lifetime working on. As anxious kids gets older, they will find more effective ways to deal with their anxiety and use the tactics they find that work the best. When I was a kid, I used exercise as a way to release my emotions. The day basketball season ended, I started looking for something else to do, not because I was bored, but because my mind/body needed it.

Over the years I have run marathons and trained for triathlons, and when my knees started suffering, I took up yoga and meditation. All of the outlets I've chosen have worked well for me; however, they have and will continue to change as I grow older. Finding a way to channel anxiety and/or emotions is just something anxious people have to learn how to do.

Once your child develops emotional awareness, he can decide how to channel his emotions. If his anxiety comes out as irritability, he can learn to go to his room until he feels better. If it comes out as energy, he can do one hundred jumping jacks before going to school in the morning, such as in Tool #13—Run Fast! Jump High! If his anxiety debilitates him physically, he can learn to take a walk or ride his bike. All of these options are important to talk over with your child.

6

Why Your Child Doesn't Need to Know about Terrorists

· ·

The picture above was drawn by a seven-year-old two weeks after 9/11. He was living in Tennessee at the time, and his picture includes bombs being launched back and forth between Tennessee and Iraq. Beside the two pieces of land are coffins listing every member of his family as having died. He's included himself in a coffin on the top left.

At the time of the drawing, the boy had been watching the coverage of 9/11 nearly every day. He had become obsessed with how the United States would retaliate to the attacks and what that would mean for him and his family. He feared World War III would break out and his home, his neighborhood, and his school would all be destroyed.

The boy had a high level of Interpersonal Intelligence and noticed how, after 9/11, his parents tensed up at the dinner table, how they stayed up late watching the news, and how they stopped talking when he entered the room. He also had a high level of Logical-Mathematical Intelligence and understood that the number of people who had died in the attacks equaled twice the number of the students at his school. As he walked around the hallways, he thought about the victims and was overcome with sadness and fear. He was also a Highly Sensitive Child and felt high amounts of empathy for those children who had lost their parents. He began thinking about what it would be like to lose his own.

This boy was not alone in his fear. Many kids across the country watched the footage of the 9/11 attacks. Whether their parents were allowing it or they just happened to be walking through the living room while the news was on, the majority of kids in the United States at that time saw a plane hit a tower at least once. For many kids, they saw planes hit towers many times, and those were often the kids who struggled the worst.

In many cases, it wasn't seeing the actual plane hit the tower that was so disturbing for kids; it was that kids really didn't understand what they were seeing. As adults, we knew we were watching a replay of what happened the morning of 9/11. Young children, however, didn't understand that. In fact, when many kids saw a plane hit a tower, they thought it was a different plane and a different tower. Thus, if a child saw a replay of a plane hitting a tower fifty times, he may have believed fifty planes had hit fifty towers. And that's where smart kids took what they were seeing to the next level.

Average Child: *Fifty planes hit fifty towers. That's a lot of towers.*

Smart Child: *Fifty planes hit fifty towers. We have towers in our city. The towers in our city will be hit next.*

The average child in the above example was experiencing concrete thinking. (*Fifty planes hit fifty towers.*) When children are thinking concretely, what they see is taken literally. Each time they see a plane hit a tower, it is seen as a separate event. It takes higher-level thinking skills (seen in children ages twelve and up) to think critically about what is seen. A critical thinker will look at the replay and think, *I recognize that event. It happened last week.* Children under eight might not able to do this.

The smart child above was experiencing both concrete thinking *(Fifty planes hit fifty towers)* and asynchronous development *(The towers in our city will be next)*. Asynchronous development caused the child to take the concrete thought to the next level by thinking his city would be next. So the average child had to deal with just concrete thinking; the smart child had to deal with both. If you take concrete thinking and add asynchronous development, you end up with a terrified child. This is what many smart kids experience when they are exposed to the realities of our world.

How Children Process World Events

If you think of a child's world in terms of a snow globe, you can see how a child views the world around him. He is in the center of a snow globe, and when it snows on him, he believes it snows on everyone. Children ages three through seven are egocentric and aren't aware of other people's perspectives. When they're having a bad day, they assume everyone else is having a bad day. When they're having a wonderful day, they assume everyone else's day is wonderful too. From a child's perspective, everything that exists, exists inside the snow globe.

For example, if a child sees a starving child on television, they see that child as in their snow globe. From their snow-globe point of view, the starving child is experiencing the same world as they are; thus, there is reason to fear they too might starve. While some kids will not be triggered by the starving child, there are many smart kids who would be. And those kids don't understand how far away Africa really is and that they have enough food in the pantry to survive for months. What they see in their world becomes part of their reality, whether it is directly related to them or not.

The same thing happens when a child sees a storm warning on television. Even if you point out that the storm is going to bypass your area altogether, a child will see the red and green flashing dots and won't be able to process the distance between himself and the storm. After all, the storm is inside their snow globe, and they can't see how it won't somehow affect them.

After 9/11, many kids assumed the buildings in their own city had been hit. When they later went downtown and saw them still standing, they were in shock. They weren't able to differentiate the towers on television from the towers in their own city, because in their snow globe, their city is all they can see. This is how their fear becomes magnified.

The same goes for kids' perception of time. Inside the snow globe, time takes on a new form. A day is like a week to a child. When you talk about what happened last week, a child will remember it like it was a long time ago. That's why it's important to address a child's behavior within the day in which it occurred, especially for children ages four through ten. Once kids get older, they gain a greater perspective of time, but for young children, if you don't address topics within the day, they will likely be forgotten.

Time also affects kids when it comes to frightening events. When a frightening event occurs, it stays stuck in the brain. If a child witnessed a house fire a year ago, when they see a candle fall off the counter and onto the floor, they will feel the same way they did when they saw the fire a year before. It's as if the fear stayed stuck in a time capsule, and when it came back, it was just as intense as it had been the first time.

How Smart Kids Fool You

Many parents say, "But my child wants to talk about the war in Iraq. He's really interested in natural disasters. He's really not afraid to watch *The Dark Knight*." They insist that their kids are smart enough to understand world events, why their marriage ended, and why they don't have enough money to pay the bills. They believe that exposing kids to adult-level information helps them understand the world more.

That perception is false.

It's not that smart kids can't understand the information, it's that they can't handle the emotional pieces that go along with it. Kids can look at your budget and see there's not enough money for dance classes. They can watch a Discovery Channel documentary and understand that polar bears are dying because of climate change. They can understand that cancer kills people and that one day it might kill you. Smart kids can understand a litany of things they emotionally can't process. As an adult, you have the capacity to understand that while you feel bad for the polar bears, they don't necessarily affect your daily life. You can go about your day and not let their survival consume you. But children can't do that. They're living in a snow globe, with the polar bears. That's why they'll spend all day trying to figure out how to help them.

Once I was working with a seven-year-old girl who was afraid of dying. She had spent hours researching information about death and knew what age the average person dies, what her chances were of being diagnosed with cancer, and how many teenagers die in car accidents. She knew all of the statistics, yet she couldn't emotionally process what death really means. Does it mean you go to heaven? Do you stay in the ground? What happens to your body?

These are questions many adults struggle with, yet in her emotional state (which was five years old), she was trying to comprehend them herself. It didn't matter how much information she had or how much her parents tried to convince her she wouldn't die, she was trying to emotionally process what most adults don't quite understand.

The Draw to Adult-Level Topics

It's hard for many parents to keep their kids away from adult information. They shield their kids from the news, keep the channel on Disney, and refrain from arguing with their spouse in front of their kids, yet their kids find ways to get adult information anyway. This is very frustrating for a parent, because you are aware of what is kid-friendly and what isn't, and you have done your best to keep your child away from the adult stuff. Even so, your child is constantly sneaking around you, trying to find access into adult things.

Many smart kids have advanced vocabularies. A few months ago,

I was working with an eight-year-old who used the word "arbitrary" in conversation. When I asked him what the word meant, he gave me the correct definition. He told me all about a "Dictionary" iPhone app that sends you a daily word and definition. Learning adult-level words excited him, and he loved having access to information kids his age couldn't understand.

The adult world is also filled with mysteries: relationships, careers, late-night phone calls, and choices. Kids don't feel they have many choices and desperately want them. "I can't wait until I can drive," an eleven-year-old told me recently. "Then I can go to the mall anytime I want." In her mind, her age is keeping her from what she really wants—to be an adolescent—so having a car will give her access to what she thinks she wants. Does she really want to deal with the academic and social pressure of being sixteen? I suppose not. However, it all seems good to her at eleven.

Smart kids are drawn to adult-level topics because:

1. **They can understand them**—The advanced intellect of smart kids gives them an option of what they choose to talk about. Since they understand many adult concepts, they can choose: *Do I want to play with the kids or talk to the adults?* Most kids don't have that option. Smart kids can jump right into the adult conversation and understand it! This option opens up a whole new world for them. If they aren't connecting with the kids at the party, they can go sit with the adults. If they are being left out or are uninterested in their friends' choice of game, they can opt out and go for the adult conversation. Many smart kids would just as soon play with their peers, but for kids who are having

trouble socially, this ability can get them out of uncomfortable social situations. When they should be figuring out how to resolve a conflict or how to find another friend, they can avoid the situation altogether by hanging out with the adults.

2. **Adult information is interesting**—Much of what kids talk about is uninteresting to smart kids. The games kids play, the arguments that occur, the way other kids react is often difficult for smart kids to process. The delicate way adults handle things is much more interesting. The way adults talk things out, the conversations they have, and their insights are very appealing to smart kids. The information itself is fascinating, especially when kids their age can't understand it. Having an edge on your peers is something all kids strive for, and for smart kids, having an edge means having more information.

3. **Adults are much better listeners**—Smart kids soak up adult conversations where they are listened to, appreciated, and validated. They also like talking about issues kids their age can't talk about. As we've learned from Chapter 1, smart kids are on a different level than their peers, and they are relieved when they can talk to someone who "gets" them. Most kids their age don't "get" them and, quite frankly, aren't good listeners. Kids their age have short attention spans and are addicted to the newest fad. If you don't have something compelling to say, they will run off and play with somebody else. This is why smart kids are drawn to adult-level topics. They finally feel like they can be a part of something, and if it means becoming interested in things adults are interested in, they'll do it.

Keeping It Kid-Friendly

Even though smart kids are drawn to adult information, it's important to keep them away from it when you can. When your child
chooses to talk to the adults at a party instead of his peers, encourage
him to go back and play with the kids. When he comes downstairs
while you are watching CNN or listens outside the door when you
are discussing your friend's wife's affair, tell him to go back to bed.
Just as you would handle it if your child wanted to eat four cupcakes
instead of just one, you set a boundary and tell him it's not allowed.

While you can't protect your child from every hardship, what you
can do is limit the information you allow them to take in. They may
be exposed to questionable things when they're not with you, but
while they're under your care, you can make decisions about what
you will and will not allow them to watch, listen to, and participate
in. After all, you never know what will trigger your child's anxiety.
Some kids were terrified by the Joplin, Missouri tornado; other kids
weren't. They may have been afraid of Friday's spelling test, but the
footage of the tornado didn't trigger their anxiety. This is just the
way things go for kids. They're triggered by different things, so it's
best to keep it "kid-friendly."

"Kid-friendly" means that what your child takes in should be
appropriate to his physical age. Just because he wants to research
tsunamis on the computer doesn't mean you should let him. If you
Google tsunamis, the search results include pictures of how tsunamis
are formed, along with thousands of images of the people who died
in Indonesia in 2004. Once a child gets those images in his head, it's
hard to get them out. Instead, screen the information your child takes
in. Checking out ten kid-level library books is a much better option

than doing ten minutes of internet research. The kid-level books will focus more on science than they do the tragedy of an event.

For example, your seven-year-old may really get into Harry Potter, which can dive into some dark issues appropriate for older children. How can he make it age-appropriate? He can order a wizard wand and go on the Harry Potter website and become a member. He can do internet research on wizardry and find out how to order a cloak for Halloween. They can take that topic to the nth degree and still be within the levels of age-appropriateness.

Kids will try to read your emails. They will try to listen to your conversations, and often times there is very little you can do about it. You can't stand over them all the time, and you can't always hide in a closet to talk on the phone. But what you can do is choose not to discuss adult information with them if they ask.

Television/Movies

Tales from the Crypt was a television show that came on late at night when I was a child. I knew better than to watch it, but once, when I had a friend over, she convinced me it wouldn't be scary. To save face, I sat through the entire episode and was so terrified I didn't sleep that night. I can still remember an image of an old woman stirring a big pot of stew with a human body inside. That image haunted me for years and, even to this day, I stay away from scary movies. My amygdala doesn't need any unnecessary triggers. Some people aren't bothered by scary movies. After watching them they fall right asleep and barely remember them the next day. I have never been that kind of person.

Anxious kids often aren't fond of scary movies either. Once

they've had a bad experience, they usually don't want anything to do with the movie or television show again. To complicate things, kids' movies today aren't what they used to be. They're very advanced. They have amazing visual effects, thanks to studios like Pixar, and can take a child to another world in an instant. However, along with those visual effects come advanced topics. As we learned from *Shrek*, if you add adult humor, adults won't mind taking their kids to the movies. So current "kids'" movies are actually targeting kids, adolescents, and adults all at the same time, and because of that, kids are being exposed to more advanced information than ever before. As a parent, you should preview the content of a movie before you let your child watch it, even if it's rated G.

If you know your child's triggers, you'll have a head start and may be able to avoid the movie if you think it may be upsetting for him. Your child may still want to go, but you should ultimately be the one to make the decision. Advertising can lure kids to see movies they shouldn't watch. They may not show their fear in the theater, but for some of them, the graphics and imagery will be the first thing they see when they shut their eyes at night.

When communicating with your child, talk about his choice of television and/or movies. If he expresses fear after watching something scary, agree that he should not watch that show anymore. Sometimes kids will do this on their own, and other times they will need you to set boundaries. Some kids think they can handle their fear and continue putting themselves in situations where they become afraid.

What can make it hard is that other kids aren't bothered by the same things. When anxious kids are at a sleepover, other kids will want to watch scary movies or tell ghost stories, and anxious kids are stuck with having to watch or listen, or leave and face the social consequences. In this case, it's important for anxious kids to try to get out of the situation by changing the subject, switching to a different movie, or leaving the room. If they can't, they need to reconsider staying the night at the same place again.

Whether it's to save face or they're trying to endure the scary parts in order to get to the good ones, you may need to step in and set boundaries for your child when he can't set them for himself.

This goes the same for television shows. Keep things kid-friendly by avoiding watching the news, adult mysteries, or shows about world events. Even if you keep the channel on Disney, there are some shows that will still be scary to some kids. Talk about these shows with your child and let him know that at the point he gets scared, he should either change the channel or leave the room. There is no sense in watching it any longer.

Phones/Computers

Most parents enjoy the luxury of having access to email and text messaging on their smartphones. That is, until their child stumbles upon their inbox and finds an email his teacher wrote in confidence, or worse yet, finds a text message about the divorce process his parents are starting.

Smart kids are fascinated with adult information. Whether it's about the birthday party you're planning or the fight you had with your spouse, smart kids like to be in the know. That's why having personal information in a place where kids can access it often leads to trouble. Quite simply, if information is on your phone, computer, or iPad, and a child has access to it, there's a chance he will read it. I've had many parents seek counseling for their child because he read something inappropriate on their phone, iPad, or computer. They are at a loss about what to tell their child because, in his current state, he knows way too much. It's hard to sugarcoat something once a child already knows the truth.

Discovering inappropriate information is a tough predicament for a child as well. His brain begins trying to process something that emotionally he can't handle. He went from being intrigued with his parents' information to being worried about money, his parents' divorce, or what his teacher had to say about his behavior at school. If he could go back and change it, he would choose not to know the information at all, because now his mind is obsessing over something he has very limited information about.

The general rule of thumb about technology is to keep your personal information away from your kids. Lock your phone. Delete your emails, and make sure anything that could be distressing to your child is put in a place they cannot access. It takes just one undeleted email or text message to change how a child views his world.

Kids and the Right to Know

Many parents fall into the trap of answering every question their child asks. They feel the need to tell their child what they were talking about on the phone, whether they can afford sleepaway camp, and whether they are really thinking about getting a divorce. *But I don't want to lie* is the belief many parents have.

The truth is: Your kids don't need to know the details of your life. It stresses them out. There is an old saying: *Don't ask questions you don't want the answers to.* Kids don't understand how this works. When questions pop into their mind, they ask them without thinking about whether they really want to know the answer.

"Mommy, are you and Daddy getting a divorce?" This is a loaded question many kids ask, especially when they hear their parents arguing. As a parent, you are backed into a corner with this question. You may know for sure you are not getting divorced, or you may be thinking about it. Regardless, your eight-year-old does not need to know about your future plans until you make a final decision.

The big question here is: Does your child really want to know if you are getting divorced? Answer: Of course not. Divorce is an adult word kids are terrified of, but since the question popped into his brain, it's coming out and landing in your lap. Do you have to answer this question? No. Should you acknowledge that your child is scared? Yes. We will discuss this topic more in the next chapter. For now, let's look at the difference between **Adult-Level** and **Kid-Level** topics.

Kid-Level Topics	Adult-Level Topics
School	College
Friends	Marriage
Conflicts on the playground	War
Allowance	Finances
Report Cards	SAT

As you can see, Kid-Level topics are often the age-appropriate counterpart to the Adult-Level topics. Kids need to talk about school; adults (or adolescents), about college. Kids need to talk about friends; adults, about marriage, and so on. When your child starts going to an Adult Level, it's time to bring them back down to the Kid Level. After all, his interest is created only out of his intellectual ability. Since smart kids are always going to the next level, it is natural for them to take the next step in going from a child conversation to an adult conversation.

When Kids Should Go to the Adult Level

Allow your child to go to an Adult Level with academics or activities. Academic topics include math, chemistry, physics, and so on. Activities include chess, karate, sports, making jewelry to sell on Etsy, etc. Allowing smart kids to completely indulge in an activity allows them to go to the next level in a healthy way. If they can play chess with older kids (or adults) or play up on the soccer team, they feel the sense of accomplishment they often need.

I worked with an extremely bright seven-year-old boy whose mother had bought a physics book and had begun teaching him the basic concepts. In fact, learning physics actually helped his anxiety, because his mind was being engaged instead of having nothing to focus on. Late at night when he couldn't sleep, he brought out a physics book and began trying to understand a new concept. Learning physics not only helped engage his mind but also helped him feel confident. He was learning something that wasn't taught in school and felt empowered.

Other parents have allowed their kids to sell their jewelry on Etsy, design clothing for dolls, and go to arts-and-crafts trade shows to check out the competition. With smart kids, everything's about the next level, so giving kids opportunities to experience the next level in healthy ways is of the utmost importance. Especially when kids have spinning mental energy, having a way to channel it will allow them to feel less anxious and to be successful as well.

When to Tell the Kids the Hard Stuff

When it comes to Adult-Level conversation, tell children only the information that will directly affect them. For example, if Dad has a drinking problem, kids need to know, so they can call the other parent before he drives them around after he's been drinking. The fact that he had several extramarital affairs is not important for them to know, unless that somehow affects the kids' emotional or physical safety. Ultimately, you don't want to lie to your kids; you just want to keep them protected.

When I was fourteen years old, my mother was diagnosed with cancer. Standing at her bedside on Christmas Eve, I thought, *My mom is going to die. This is going to be the last Christmas with my mother.* Despite what the doctors said, and despite what my mother even told me herself, I believed: cancer = death. During that time, I jumped to thinking like an adult. I started working out in my mind who would do the laundry, who would cook the meals, and who would help my sister with her homework. I wasn't old enough to drive, so I planned for my brother to take us grocery shopping and that we'd have to be sure to get plenty of green beans and 2% milk at the store. Since my dad had to work, we'd have to take care of the house, and it was my job to make sure everyone had what they needed. It wasn't until my mother fully recovered that I let go of my ideas of how things had to be with her gone.

Many kids younger than fourteen have to deal with the death of a parent. They may also have to deal with an illness of their own or a death of a sibling. Life does not spare children great trauma, and many kids, anxious or not, have to deal with things they aren't emotionally equipped for. Life for these kids will forever be changed.

Still, when a parent is terminally ill or a child faces an illness himself, the truth is always better than a made-up story. When these tragedies exist, it's important to be honest with kids about what has happened or might happen. For example, if a child has cancer, it's important to let siblings know he is seriously ill and doesn't just have the flu. In cases such as death or illness, hospitals are often equipped with child-life specialists to help children process what is happening to themselves or within their family.

But if kids don't have to deal with traumatic events, why should they be exposed to them? If they are lucky enough to avoid losing a parent, why should they be exposed to death? If they are lucky enough not to lose their home in a tsunami, why should they be exposed to the devastation? Quite frankly, they shouldn't.

The Shortened Childhood

Many parents are shocked by how advanced their children are. Even if they try to keep things "kid-friendly," their kids are developing teenage interests and behaviors as young as seven and eight years old. Their kids are acting like teenagers, arguing like teenagers, and manipulating their parents like teenagers.

Why is this happening?

Many of the behavior changes in kids can be attributed to the media. Today's television programs encourage children to talk back to their parents by making it seem funny. Even cartoons now include sassy behavior and words such as "whatever," "yeah, right," and "duh" and are being viewed over and over again by kids across America. Kids are seeing these behaviors as funny and cute and are trying them out on their parents because they seem to work so well on television.

What kids don't learn from the media or from their older siblings, they will learn from other kids on the playground. Even if you keep your kids from watching SpongeBob, another child's parents will allow their kids to watch it, and their child will tell your child about it on the playground. You can't avoid this, and even if you try, kids love to talk about teenage things to have access to what the older kids are doing.

Recent research has proven that instead of kids just talking about adolescent things at a younger age, today's kids are actually physically developing earlier than kids have in the past.

In 2010, *Pediatrics* journal published a study that 15 percent of girls are now beginning puberty by age seven. They also found that one in ten girls began developing breasts by age seven, twice the rate seen in a 1997 study. Sandra Steingraber, author of a 2007 report on early puberty for the Breast Cancer Fund said, "Over the last thirty years, we've shortened the childhood of girls by a year and a half." It's not clear what is causing this change, but regardless, it is a biological fact.

So what parents are seeing is not made up or false. Going by the above study alone, if you have a daughter at age thirty, she will develop a year and a half sooner than you did. A year and a half is a long time when you consider how short childhood is anyway. When you add the advancement of technology and the media, you can see why today's kids look like little adults. An important part of childhood is believing the world is safe and you are protected. Today's kids are feeling less and less protected and, because of their rapid development, are thrown into a world they aren't ready for.

Being a kid is tough. No longer are kids sheltered from the tragedies of the world; they can find them all with a click of a button. Here are some ideas on how to prevent technology from tainting your child's good, old-fashioned childhood.

4 Ways to Preserve Childhood

1. **Get a parental block on your computer.** Even if you have a five-year-old and a seven-year-old at home, you never know when a sleepover will lead to late-night computer searching. You never know when your child will hear the word "death" or "sex" at school and come home and do a Google search. Parental blocks will shield your children from the vast amount of information they have no business accessing and can be put on with a simple call to your internet company.

2. **Censor what you watch in front of your kids.** This seems obvious, but many parents spend their evenings watching the news or movies their kids shouldn't see. Even if your child says, "It's okay. I'm not scared," don't believe it. The G rating is there for a reason. Stick to it. Some kids will even get scared watching G-rated movies, and if this is the case, give your child an out. Tell your child it's okay to be scared, and he can leave the room at any point, no questions asked.

3. **Watch what you say in front of your child.** This not only includes arguing with your spouse but also talking about Adult-Level things in front of your child. Talking about money is a

prime example of how simple conversations can cause kids to worry. While you want your child to understand the value of a dollar, there is no need to explain your issues with money. Explaining that the family can't go to the beach because Dad lost his job is not productive. Saying you're choosing to go on a camping trip instead is a much better scenario. Kids will have the rest of their lives to worry about money. Childhood is not the time.

4. **Let your kids be kids.** I can't tell you how many times I've heard kids say they don't play. "You don't play?!?" I ask, looking around my room filled with toys. I am a play therapist, after all, and know that kids largely work out their issues by playing. "I'm not really into it," they say before I introduce them to a tray of Moon Sand. By the second session, the kid is making castles, laughing, and creating his own world in the sand tray. By nature, kids are designed to play. They're also designed to create and imagine. If your child would rather sit in the kitchen and talk with you while you cook, encourage him to go outside and play with friends. Encourage play dates and sleepovers, even if they're with older or younger kids. Connecting with other kids is important for social development, even if it's hard at first. As a parent, you can't control when your child goes through puberty. You can't control what they hear on the playground or when they develop teenage behaviors. What you can do, however, is try to protect them to the best of your ability. Control what they watch when they're in your house, control what you talk about in front of them, and don't allow them to pull adult information out of you without taking time to think about your response.

7

How to Answer "Is Global Warming Real? When Will I Die? Can a Tornado Hit Our House?" ...and Other Tough Questions

· ·

A s a parent, you don't have to answer all of your child's questions. You are not required to answer them, nor are you necessarily going to make a tough situation better if you do. "Mommy, when will I die?" is a question kids will ask. "Uh…well…we just… uh…" is all many parents can come up with. Kids will throw you off, so it's important to understand why kids ask questions in the first place and how you can give appropriate answers to even the toughest questions.

Why Kids Ask Questions

"Can I have another snack?" "What time are we leaving?" "I'm hungry. When is dinner?" "Can I go outside?" These are the questions kids ask day after day, for years on end. Why? Because kids are constantly needing permission. Because they're kids, they can't cook their own dinner, make their own cookies, or cross the street alone. They need their parent to "okay" everything they do.

Kids also ask questions about abstract things that pique their interest. The questions can be about world events, adult issues, or concepts that seem completely random. For example, "Can dinosaurs come back on the Earth? What if all the mummies in Egypt woke up? Will I see Grandma when I die? If God made everything, who made God?" These questions come out of the blue and are the most difficult for parents to answer.

There are three main reasons why kids ask these kinds of questions:

1. *They are curious.*
2. *They don't understand something.*
3. *They are seeking comfort.*

Kids are curious. With their ever-expanding brains, kids are constantly taking in new information. They are learning how the world works and turn to you for answers. They want to know why the grass is green, why daddy long-legs spiders don't bite, and why the Earth is round. Kids fall into a pattern of asking questions because they're continually in the role of not knowing something. At school, the teacher knows the answers. At home, parents know the answers. Kids become dependent on the adults in their lives to tell them what to do and how things work.

In my office, I have shelves of miniatures. When I first start seeing kids, many of them will pick up a very recognizable miniature and ask me what it is. For example, a child will pick up a dog and ask, "What's this?" When I say, "It can be whatever you want it to be," the child says, "It's a dog," and moves on. The child didn't need me to tell him what it was. In fact, what he needed was for me *not* to tell him what it was. He needed to make his own decision. That simple question/answer sequence was the first step in helping him become more independent.

Other kids will immediately ask for help rather than trying something on their own. If they're playing in the sand, they will hand me the bucket and ask me to make the sand castle. Kids who immediately ask for help are often perfectionists who have a low frustration tolerance. Because they know you can build a better sand castle (because you're an adult), they will defer to you rather than going through the process of building it themselves. While an adult can indeed build it better and quicker, kids who receive help don't get to feel the full reward of feeling successful on their own.

If your child is in the habit of asking questions he already knows the answer to, try putting the question back on him. If he asks what time dinner is, you can say, "What time do we usually have dinner?" If he asks what time you're leaving for school, take him to a clock and show him what time you will be leaving each day. Say, "When the big hand gets on the six, we will be leaving for school." The next time he asks you, remind him that he already knows.

If your child is in the habit of asking you to do things he could easily do himself, set a timer for three to five minutes and tell him you will help him after he's tried doing it himself. If he quits, then you'll know it wasn't that important to him in the first place. When he asks for help, instead of saying, "You can do that by yourself," (which encourages him to say "No, I can't") say, "I know you would like for me to help you. After you try your best for five minutes, I will help you." Often times, by the time the timer goes off, kids will have figured things out on their own. If this is the case, make a big deal out of it. Say, "You did that all by yourself. I'm so proud of you." This allows your child to feel the success he wouldn't have felt had you simply stepped in and helped him.

They don't understand something. This is why you hear kids ask "why" all the time. They don't understand why they have to get dressed, why they have to stop playing, and why they have to go to bed. Kids don't understand social norms (being dressed in public is expected) and developmental norms (kids should get plenty of sleep), so they ask you, "Why, why, why."

To seek comfort. This is the number-one reason anxious kids ask questions, and it puts parents in a tough position, because no matter how you respond, it doesn't seem to make a difference. You can tell your child fifty times that he still has to go to the dentist, but that doesn't stop him from asking a fifty-first time. When kids are seeking comfort, they will ask the same question over and over again. Instead of processing the answer you've already given them, they will ask the question again as a way to release their spinning mental energy. These questions are usually based on a few different scenarios:

1. **If something is going to happen** (death, tornadoes, earthquakes, the end of the world). Anxious kids spend hours worrying about things that will never happen. Whether it's something they've heard about or seen on the news, kids who live in landlocked states will worry about hurricanes, and kids who live in the desert will worry about blizzards. They will worry about anything that triggers their anxiety. Kids will also worry about things that really could happen, such as whether the storm warning will turn into a tornado or whether their cat with a large

tumor on his back will die. Regardless, when kids are worried about something, they will ask repetitive questions as a way to soothe their minds.

2. **If they're going to have to do something** (sleepaway camp, soccer tournament, piano recital). Future events are tough on anxious kids. When they know something is coming up, they will begin worrying about it weeks or even months in advance. Future events are all about the unknown and when anxious kids start playing out scenarios in their mind, they always see the worst. If it's May and they know they will be going to sleepaway camp in July, anxious kids may waste the first half of the summer worrying about what will happen at sleepaway camp. "Do I have to go? Please don't make me. Can't I just go next year?" If this sounds like your child, pay special attention to Tool #4: The Five Question Rule and Tool #12: Brain Plate. The Five Question Rule will help you set boundaries, while Brain Plate will help teach your child how to stay in the present and focus on one day at a time.

How to Answer 90 Percent of Tough Questions

The hardest part about a child's questions is that you don't know how to answer many of them. "Will a tornado hit our house? Is global warming real? Will a tsunami hit the beach we're staying at? Can kids get so sick they die?" These are nightmare questions for parents, because there are no set answers. If you answer "no," you aren't really telling the truth. If you answer "yes," you may frighten your child even more.

Many parents tell their kids too much because, as children, their parents didn't tell them enough. A parent I worked with was traumatized when her own mother didn't tell her she had cancer and then died six months later. When she became a parent herself, she vowed to always be honest with her kids so when her eleven-year-old boy asked if she could die during a minor surgery, she said, "Yes, I could die. Anyone could die during surgery." Her son was devastated and began obsessing over his mother's health. Essentially, her plan to keep her kids in the know backfired, because she went from one extreme to the other.

There were things our parents did in all of our childhoods that make us want to do things differently. It's no wonder people often go from one extreme to the other, hoping not to "mess up" their kids like they felt their parents did. If your parents told you nothing, you may tend to tell your child too much. If your parents told you too much, you may tend not to tell your child enough about what's going on.

For example, it's not uncommon for parents to tell their children that one parent is at "camp" when they're really in rehab or prison. While kids understand what "camp" is, the next time they have an opportunity to go to summer camp themselves, they'll be terrified. They'll think they have to be away for a long time and that "camp" will make them feel sad. Thus, the idea of "camp," though it was a kid-friendly word, ends up confusing some kids in the long run.

If you find yourself in the position of either 1) feeling pressured to answer your child's questions or 2) feeling pressured to tell your child more than he's emotionally prepared for, follow the three steps below. They will allow you to field most questions with responses that not only give kids what they need but will empower them as well.

1. **Acknowledge the Feeling**—This is the most important part of answering a question, because it gets to the heart of why the question is being asked in the first place. "Daddy, is there a tornado coming?" is a typical question an anxious child will ask. If you simply say, "No, sweetie. There's nothing to worry about," you'll miss the point of your daughter's question. She's asking the question because she is scared and wants to know you'll take care of her. She doesn't know enough about tornadoes to know if one's really coming, nor does she know how to handle the situation if one does occur. She just needs you to acknowledge how she feels and to let her know you're there for her. By saying, "I know you're scared, and I'm here for you," you get to the heart of her concern and address it. You also help raise her emotional intelligence by acknowledging her feeling, which helps her become more aware of herself. The response also gets you out of the position of determining whether a tornado will hit your house. After all, you cannot say with any degree of certainty what will and will not happen when it comes to the weather.

2. **Ask Open-Ended Questions**—When you ask open-ended questions, you discover more about how your child is feeling. You begin to understand his fears, and when you understand them you will be much more useful in your approach. An example of an open-ended question is "What part of a tornado scares you?" The answer seems obvious, but kids will surprise you. "I'm afraid the dog will be swept away" is a common answer. You

had no idea this was your child's fear. If you bring your boxer, Rocky, into the house, your child might suddenly feel better. Open-ended questions help both you and your child pinpoint where the fear lies. When you assume what a child is worried about, you target a fear that is not really there. If you say, "Our house is made out of brick; there's no way it will fall down," a child may develop a new fear of the house blowing over when he didn't even know that was an option. Open-ended questions clarify where the fear lies so you can address your child's fears directly without creating new fears along the way.

3. **Avoid Giving Concrete Answers**—Kids come to parents wanting answers 100 percent of the time. They want a "yes" or a "no" or a specific answer to their question, and many parents feel they have to give their children what they want. There's a difference between what children want and what they need, and as a parent you have to decide what you are willing to give them. Henry Ford said, "If I'd asked people what they wanted, they would have said faster horses," and when it comes to kids, giving your child what he wants is not necessarily the best option. It's not that you shouldn't address your child's question, but simply saying if something will or will not happen is often not a good choice. Once you say something won't happen, and then later it does happen, your child will no longer trust you. If you say your child won't have to get braces, and he finds out a year later he has to, then he will see you as dishonest. If you tell him he won't have to get a shot, and he ends up getting one, he will not only distrust you but be filled with anger.

Here's an example of how concrete answers cause problems:

Daughter: "Daddy, will a tornado destroy our house?"
Dad: "No, sweetie, of course not."
Daughter: "How do you know?"
Dad: "Tornadoes don't destroy houses."
Daughter: "What about those people on TV? How come their houses got destroyed?"

Now you're stuck. You can either go on explaining (or trying to explain), or you can stop and start over. Look at how differently this conversation plays out.

Daughter: "Daddy, will a tornado hit our house?"
Dad: "You seem really scared right now."
Daughter: "Yeah, I'm afraid of tornadoes."
Dad: "I see that. What part scares you the most?"
Daughter: "The wind knocking our house down."
Dad: "That does sound scary. What do you think might make you feel better?"
Daughter: "If you close the curtains."
Dad: "Of course. I can do that."

This conversation works much better, because the child is actually processing her fears instead of just dumping them on her father. She has to think about what might make her feel better instead of requiring her parent to jump in and rescue her. Parents will often rescue kids by saying things like, "There's nothing to worry about.

We're safe. Nothing bad is going to happen," but these comments only promote arguing. Kids don't believe there's nothing to worry about, because their minds and bodies are telling them differently. To them, there is a lot to worry about, and they need to find a way to feel better. Kids aren't good at saying, "Daddy, I'm scared. Please help me feel safe." They're better at saying, "Will a tornado hit our house?" But the statements essentially mean the same thing.

When kids process their fears themselves, they learn how to identify their own triggers. If they process all of their anxiety through you, they don't learn anything. The girl in the example needed to learn that closing the curtains would make her feel better. Now that she knows, she won't be so dependent on her father. If her parents are in another part of the house, she can shut the curtains on her own without needing them to soothe her. Ultimately, she will be able to soothe herself during an anxious time. This ability to self-soothe is what gives anxious kids the confidence to face scary situations.

How to Answer the Other 10 Percent of Questions

There are times when you are so caught off guard you can't go through the three steps. You are on the way to soccer practice, cooking for a dinner party, or taking the kids to school when WHAM! your child asks, "What happens when you die?" While the timing seems completely random, often it's not. Kids feel safer asking questions when you're busy. When you're not looking at them or are occupied with something else, it feels safer, because you're giving them less attention.

Kids also ask questions at bad times because they can't not ask them. They're feeling things so intensely they have no choice but to talk about them. My middle of the night "I don't want to have a baby" conversation with my mother was a prime example of this. The fear was so big I couldn't not talk about it. It had been spinning in my mind so long it had to come out.

Especially right before anxiety-producing events, kids will either want to talk about fears at bedtime or will have a hard time sleeping. The end of the day is the hardest time for anxious kids because their minds aren't actively engaged. When smart kids don't have something to occupy their minds, their minds will spin anyway, often picking up new things to worry about or going back to Default Worries. That's why anxious kids will call you back to their bedroom five times or try to get you to stay until they fall asleep. When they're left alone, their minds get the best of them. While you're there to comfort them, they can become relaxed enough to fall asleep.

Their spinning minds will also wake them up in the middle of the night. They may fall asleep in their own bed, but you'll find them lying next to you when you wake up the next morning. They may tell you about a bad dream they had or say something scared them. Most often, however, it's their spinning mind that woke them up. Because they didn't want to be afraid any longer, they sought comfort from you.

Whether it's in the middle of the night or on the way to school, kids will ask questions to release mental pressure. To answer these 10 percent of questions, try using **the Five-Minute Rule**, **Fleeting Questions,** and **Joining In**:

1. **The Five-Minute Rule**—When kids catch you off guard with a question, buy yourself time by saying, "I'm sorry, but I can't give you my full attention right now. I can talk to you about that in five minutes." If you need more time, say ten minutes, fifteen minutes, however long you need to collect your thoughts and answer in the most effective way possible. This not only buys you time but also allows the question to leave the child's mind. Often, kids will get distracted with something else and lose interest in finding out the answer. If kids do come back to the question, give them an answer that's on their level. If you've already given them an age-appropriate answer, stick with it by becoming a broken record. If you haven't talked about the issue before, try and figure out where the question is coming from. For example, if they ask about death, instead of going into a long spiel, say "What have you heard?" or "What would you like to know?" This will help you understand where they're coming from instead of making assumptions that will lead you to a more advanced conversation than is really warranted.

2. **Fleeting Questions**—If you delay answering a child's question, they will often forget about it. Thus, some of your child's toughest questions will simply go away. Tool #2: Worry Time addresses fleeting questions directly. If your child asks lots of questions, chances are what's coming out of his mouth will be forgotten much of the time. If your child is not a big talker, he may be more apt to wait for the answer, but if you put the question off for at least five minutes, most kids will move on to something else.

Smart kids' minds are fast, so don't stress yourself out by trying to answer a question that will just go away. Instead, delay the answer and wait to see if your child's question comes back. If it does, say, "I remember you asking that question before. You really seem to want to know the answer." Then decide if you want to answer the question or not.

Quite often, a perfectly good answer is "I don't know," because, in reality, you won't know how to answer many of the questions your child asks. Responding with "I don't know" not only lets you off the hook, but also allows kids to come up with answers on their own.

One parent of a difficult child insists that she only responds to 25 percent of her child's questions. "Mommy, can we go outside now?" her daughter will ask, and only on the fourth time will her mother respond. Her response is then, "I heard you the other three times, and no, we will not be able to go outside right now." This mother is very laid-back, and her daughter is very high-strung, so this situation works out well for both parties. Because the mother is relaxed, when her daughter is pounding her with questions, she remains calm and consistent.

This approach is not as easy for many parents. Often, both parent and child are reactive, so by the fourth time a child asks a question, the parent is frustrated. If you have the patience to try this approach, it often works beautifully. Because you aren't responding to everything your child throws out, it gives your child a chance to redirect himself or to move on to something else. It also teaches your child that you will not respond to everything he says, especially if he is repeating himself. After all, some questions aren't worth answering.

3. **Joining In**—Most parents try to be strong for their kids. When their kids are worried about something, parents try to make them feel better by saying "There's nothing to worry about" or "That's not scary" or "Everything will be okay." Essentially, they are trying to convince their child that their fear is irrational. While this sounds like a logical approach, it's important to understand that anxiety does not come from the rational mind. Anxiety comes from the irrational mind, so logic doesn't work. You can't rationalize with someone who is being irrational.

A better approach is to normalize your child's fears. When you acknowledge the fear and say it's okay to be afraid, you team up with your child. When you say something is not scary or he shouldn't be afraid, you separate from him emotionally, making your disconnection even greater. When you join him, he feels connected and is more able to calm his fear.

A good example of this: I was working with a boy who developed a strong fear of parking garages. He complained about how dark and creepy they were, and every time his mother would pull inside one, he became terrified. His mother spent many weeks trying to talk him out of his fears by saying parking garages were safe and there was nothing to be worried about, but her encouragement didn't make him less afraid. It actually intensified his fear. When you try to convince kids that something isn't scary, it only increases the struggle. Before, he was struggling only with parking garages; now, he's struggling with parking garages and his mother trying to convince him they're not scary.

When I found out the approach his mother was using, I suggested she try something else. Instead of trying to convince him there was nothing to worry about, I suggested she admit that parking garages are creepy and that she doesn't like going in them either. The next time they got ready to pull inside a parking garage, his mother pulled to the side of the road. She said, "I wanted you to know I think parking garages are creepy too. I don't like them either, so after we finish up with the appointment, let's get ice cream to reward ourselves for being brave." They continued talking about everything they despised about parking garages and ended up having fun with it. They pointed out the spider webs in the corners and how the ceilings are low and how the car sounds louder inside than it does outside. The approach worked beautifully, because instead of struggling with her son, his mother joined him. Her son felt understood and safe, and when they pulled out of the parking garage that day, they went for an ice cream.

Haven't I Heard This Before?

Kids' questions often go in cycles. They ask about death, then they switch to tornadoes, then growing old, then they go back to death again. When kids go in cycles, it's important to point this out to them. Saying things like "You were asking about this last summer" will help kids get perspective on their worries.

Anxiety is a mental fog kids can't see through. When they ask about death, they forget they may have already resolved the issue in the past. They had decided that people go to heaven when they die, but the worry has come back again. When you say, "You were asking about that last summer," it's a good idea to include, "Remind me what you thought about it then." This helps kids learn to answer their own questions rather than relying on you to answer for them. When they can come up with their own solutions, they learn how to solve their own anxiety.

Questions and Power Struggles

Kids will also use questions to bait their parents. When their emotional tanks are full, they will use questions to lure their parents into a struggle. "Can I play on the computer?" is a question many kids will ask multiple times a day. They know what the answer is going to be, yet they ask the question anyway. That's partially because they want to go play on the computer and partially because when they wake up feeling angsty, they search for a way to release their emotions and bait you into a conversation that will cause a meltdown.

If you find yourself in this position, set a rule about playing on the computer (or whatever the question is based on) and stick with it. Choose a certain time of day he will be able to play on the computer, and when your child asks you the question, put the question back on him by saying, "What time do you get to play on the computer?" This will help you get out of the habit of saying "no" to your child.

It's not that "no" should never come out of your mouth, but if you find yourself saying "no, no, no," you are likely answering questions you don't need to be answering. You are also giving your child a perfect chance to empty his emotional tank without having to process his own emotions. Rest assured, it's not really about the computer or Legos or American Girl dolls. It's about anxiety and emotion and irritability.

Especially with strong-willed kids, asking questions can be a huge way to try to gain control. When they ask you a question they know you will say "no" to, they immediately start a power struggle. If you bite the bait, they will try and manipulate you into saying "yes" or have a meltdown over you saying "no." That's why it's good to take a step back and ask yourself:

1. *Did I already answer this question?*
2. *Does this question warrant an answer?*
3. *Is my child trying to bait me?*

This should allow you to take a more rational approach. Rather than giving an answer that will cause an argument or repeating yourself over and over again, take a moment to gain perspective, then proceed.

How to Respond to Tough Comments

Kids not only ask tough questions, they make tough comments. They talk bad about the other parent, say you don't love them as much as their sibling, and that you never listen to them when they need you to. When kids say these things, do not try to convince them otherwise. Chances are, they don't really mean them, and when you investigate their comment too much, it gives it more power.

Start by asking yourself: *Is my child angry?* If the answer is "yes," then you are most likely dealing with an issue of anger instead of an issue of reality. The child's anger has fogged up the lens of reality, and he is seeing things differently than he does in a normal situation. Kids say an array of hurtful things when they're angry, and once they calm down, they often apologize and feel guilty. They'll want to cuddle up with you, say they love you, and search for a way to be emotionally close again. Over time, this anger/guilt cycle takes a toll on a child's self-esteem. This is how the cycle usually goes for kids:

Say awful things → Feel guilty about saying those awful things → Try to make up with parent → Hope parent forgets those awful things → Parent lectures about the awful things that were said = *I can't believe I said those awful things. I'm a bad person.*

Over time, kids start seeing themselves in a negative light. They start to see themselves as "bad" or "awful" just because they said and did "awful" things.

Instead, emotionally disengage and respond to your child's comments with a neutral response such as: "Really?" Let's look at the examples below:

Example #1:
Son: "Mommy, I know you love Joseph more than me."
Mom: "Why would you say that? I love you both the same!"
Son: "Because you never make Joseph pick up his toys."
Mom: "Yes I do! I make Joseph pick up his toys all the time."
Son: "No you don't. You love him more!"

If you engage at the emotional level of your child, you will exacerbate the situation. Your child is angry and baiting you into a conversation that's on the level of anger. Of course you don't love your other son more, so there's no need to defend yourself. If your son says he feels you love his brother more when he is not angry, then you can discuss the issue, because then it is valid. If he says it only when he's angry, chances are he is just pushing your buttons.

Let's look at how this conversation goes when you respond with "Really?":

Example #2
Son: "Mommy, you love Joseph more than me."
Mom: "Really?"
Son: "Yes! You never make Joseph pick up his toys."
Mom: "I'm sorry you feel that way."

This response takes the power out of the situation. The boy is trying to bait his mother, and she's not falling for it. She connects with him by saying she's sorry he feels that way, but she's not willing to be emotionally dragged down to his mental state. If her son brings up the issue when he's not angry or if it becomes a constant theme, then she should address it when he is calm and open to talking about his feelings. Again, it's not necessary for her to defend herself by going through a slew of reasons why she loves her kids the same. It's more important to hear what her son is saying and accept it for what it is. If she becomes defensive, her child will likely become more offensive.

The Importance of Self-Soothing

When kids ask repetitive questions and you give them repetitive answers, they don't learn how to self-soothe. Self-soothing is the ability to cope with uncomfortable emotions and is what many smart kids are lacking. They are smart enough to understand advanced topics, but they don't know how to deal with negative emotions surrounding them.

Here is an example:

Francesca has Relational Anxiety, and anytime something goes wrong at school, she gets in the car and cries. Day after day she complains that someone said something mean, that she doesn't have any friends, and that the teacher does nothing to help her. Her mother is always there to pick her up after school and talk about the situation. Her mother listens, asks questions, and makes suggestions, but things are not getting any better. In fact, they are getting worse. Francesca is stuck in her anxiety, and her mother has become so concerned about her daughter that she's joined her at the same level of defeat.

Why isn't Francesca's anxiety getting better? The first problem is that Francesca and her mother have gotten into a pattern of anxiety. At the end of every day, Francesca knows her mother is going to ask how her day went, and Francesca will have her mother's full attention as long as she's talking about her problems. Full attention is what every child wants; however, full attention is helpful to children only when it's at the level of connection. Francesca and her mother are meeting at a place of anxiety, rather than a place of connection.

Secondly, Francesca's mother is so invested in the dynamic between Francesca and her friends that she is losing sight of the bigger picture. Because she's spent much of her day worrying about Francesca, Francesca can sense her mother's anxiety when she picks her up and is feeding off of it. Instead of being relaxed when she picks her up, Francesca's mother is tense, and her emotions are palpable. She desperately wants Francesca to have friends, and the fact that she doesn't is devastating her.

Here's what will help:

1. **Mom needs to be calm when she picks Francesca up.** She should take deep breaths, listen to relaxing music, and realize she cannot control how her daughter's day went. The most important thing she can do is be present and calm when her daughter gets into the car.

2. **Mom should avoid asking questions about how things went with Francesca's friends.** Initially, Mom should avoid asking Francesca questions at all. Instead, she should say, "Hi, Francesca. It's good to see you." If Francesca doesn't report anything, Mom should refrain from asking about her day and move on to what her after-school activities include. If Francesca brings up anxiety about friends, her mother should refer to Step 3.

3. **Set up Worry Time (Tool #2).** If Francesca brings up her worries, Mom can say, "I really want to hear about this, but I want to give you my full attention. Let's talk about this at 6:00 tonight when I can really listen to what you have to say."

As soon as Mom lets go of the anxiety and changes the situation, Francesca will start learning how to self-soothe. Since the pattern is already in place for Francesca to report about her day, she's depending on it. When Mom doesn't allow it until later in the day, it helps Francesca learn to cope with her emotions until the set time.

It also helps Francesca and her mother connect on different levels rather than just the level of anxiety. They can talk about other things and celebrate the good parts of the day without obsessing about the bad ones. This also teaches kids to see the gray areas where they usually see situations only as black/white. They see their day as all good/all bad, but when you point out both the good and the bad, kids learn to assimilate their days. Blanket Tool (Tool #9) is a great way to help kids with black/white thinking, as it helps kids process the events of their whole day rather than just the bad parts.

Learning from Past Mistakes

Many parents come into my office feeling defeated and overwhelmed because they may have handled their child's questions poorly. "I was just so frustrated I snapped," a mother said recently after telling her child that yes, they are tight on money and that is due to the fact that her father left and she had to go back to work. "I was just tired of hearing her ask why we can't go to the beach for vacation like we usually do, and now she's worried about money." I helped her, along with many other parents over the years, understand that she is human and will not always answer her child's questions the right way. What's important is to recognize your mistake and learn from it. Once you have said something you regret, try not to get caught in the same trap again.

Kids, after all, will go through periods of asking certain questions and then move on to something else. Instead of spending time regretting what you've said wrong, focus on what you said right and build on it. Think about the times you were able to come up with a great response and what made the difference for you that time. Were you rested? Able to give your full attention? Not stressed out yourself? Whatever the conditions were, try and set up those same conditions so you will have better chances of success in the future.

8

What Anxiety Leaves Behind

• •

Anxiety does get better. For some kids, it happens in a few weeks, and for others, it may take months. Given the right tools, anxious kids will feel empowered, and their anxiety will lessen. They'll be able to handle the things they weren't able to handle before and will have more good days than bad. When this happens, both kids and their parents are relieved. "I feel like I have my child back," is what many parents say after their anxious child stops worrying. Kids themselves will say, "My worries are gone!" and will feel a huge sense of relief. While having an anxiety-free child is blissful, it doesn't mean life from here on out will be a piece of cake.

When anxiety goes away, anxious kids begin to smile again. They seem light and happy and say things like "I'm not worried anymore" or "That doesn't scare me like it used to." It's a momentous time for kids, because they feel so much better. It's as if the sun has come out and all is well in their world. Even if kids don't say it themselves, parents can tell when anxiety loosens its grip. They see their kids relax, their moods lift, and their irritability go away. When anxiety breaks, kids seem better than ever, and some parents are under the impression that anxiety is gone for good.

The Streak of Bliss

When anxiety breaks, kids are on cloud nine and the world couldn't be a better place. And for kids, this can happen rather quickly. Adults can take weeks, months, even years to feel better, whereas kids can feel better in a fraction of that time. Once a child turns the corner, they leave anxiety in the dust, at least for the time being. In my office, the turnaround can happen within one week. I may have been seeing a child for five weeks (one session per week) with little to no change in his anxiety, and then suddenly it's gone. Either he's implemented a tool that worked magically or something else has taken place. That something is often a mystery.

Parents continually say, "I don't know what's changed, but he just isn't worrying anymore." This is usually a "thin ice" period of time where parents feel like things could fall apart again at any minute. However, once a child has been anxiety-free for several weeks or months, he will build enough confidence to get through anxious moments without being thrown off track. Overcoming anxiety helps kids feel better about their ability to cope. They stop worrying so much about future events and feel more confident about their ability to control their fear. But what exactly has taken place? What made the anxiety go away? For each child it's different. Let's look at the possibilities: Anxiety-reduction tools, relationship to counselor/therapist, adjustments in parenting, and a team approach are all important to a child getting better.

If your child has already gone through the counseling process, you may be able to identify what factor made the most difference. If he hasn't, you may need to look at each of these factors and decide for yourself. In my experience, all of the factors above make a child's anxiety decrease. It isn't just the tools or the counselor. It isn't just adjustments in parenting or that the child's teacher was involved. When you start addressing your child's anxiety, you will find it takes making changes on several different levels to see lasting effects. Some factors may be more important than others, but when everything comes together, kids can get better rather quickly.

Bumps in the Road

Once your child's anxiety has broken, I would encourage you to celebrate but also to be aware that for most kids, an undercurrent of anxiety will remain. It may be subtle, but it will still be there to some extent and will probably come back in the future. But this time, you will be more prepared. You will have the tools to know how to handle it, and so will your child. A child's first bout with anxiety is usually the worst. The anxiety that follows may still be intense, but since a child has experienced it before, it won't be as debilitating. What generally happens is that kids get better, and then they are exposed to something scary and they begin feeling anxious again. It's not as bad as the first time, but after having a bad dream, they start worrying again. This is considered a bump in the road and not a reason to panic.

Bumps in the road are nothing more than old triggers reappearing briefly in a child's life. They give kids a chance to use the tools they've been taught and parents a chance to use their own tools. Together with his parents, the child will be able to get through the anxious time. Some kids come back to therapy during this time, and other kids don't; it just depends on how serious the anxiety is. One thing to be leery of is running back to therapy whenever something negative comes up, as it sends a message that the child cannot handle his anxiety alone. If you feel like your child has been struggling especially hard and needs some extra support, call the therapist. If not, allow your child to be empowered by his ability to handle the anxiety on his own.

Over the course of your child's life, there will be many bumps in the road. It may be a change in friend groups or being cut from a sports team, but bumps in the road are part of childhood and are actually a good thing for kids to go through. Childhood is the time where kids have a chance to experiment with life within the safety of a parental boundary. When children are young, parents set up boundaries around them that slowly become larger over time. In Michael Riera's book titled *Staying Connected to your Teenager*, he talks about parents going from "managers" to "consultants" as their kids get older. When children are young, parents play a more active role in protecting them, but as they get older, parents slowly release control so kids have an opportunity to make their own choices. If the boundaries become too large too quickly, kids will feel unsafe, and if they remain too small, kids will suffer from being sheltered. The key is to slowly extend the boundaries so kids can fall, skin their knees, and still receive comfort from the parents along the way.

Over time, the boundaries will expand until kids go away to college and experience life on their own. At that stage, kids will come back inside the safety of the parental relationship only when the world is too scary and they need to. Ideally, by the time kids go to college, they won't need to lean on their parents nearly as much as they did in high school. Similarly, if kids can learn to manage the bumps in the road, they should be less and less dependent on parents and therapists to help manage them.

Irritability

Many parents leave my office with an anxiety-free child only to come back with an irritable child. Parents aren't sure where the irritability has come from and assume the irritability has replaced their child's anxiety, which is not really the case. What happened was that when their child's anxiety went away, the irritability was exposed. It's not that irritability replaced their child's anxiety; it's that irritability had been hiding behind the anxiety.

Irritability is the ability to become easily annoyed or angered, and in the *DSM* irritability is actually listed as a symptom of anxiety. When a child is anxious, however, irritability is often overlooked because anxiety is causing the most disruption. Anxious kids refuse to go places and do things, wreaking havoc on family schedules and daily routines. Once anxiety improves, irritability is exposed and often makes things equally difficult. Instead of kids being afraid to go places, now they just don't want to go places, and parents find themselves in the same hopeless positions they were in when their child was anxious.

Irritability generally sets in after a brief period of anxiety-free bliss. Once kids feel better, their mood immediately improves, but what they eventually settle back into is not exactly blissful. In fact, anxious kids who aren't experiencing acute anxiety can be extremely impatient and reactive. If things don't go their way, they are quick tempered. This can lead to tantrums or yelling in an effort to get their way as soon as possible. The same surge that filled them with anxiety is the same surge that comes into play when they are not getting their way, when they're hungry, or are not getting their needs met. Whether they're reacting to a scary thought or a bad dream, the same emotional surge you see during a bout of anxiety is the same surge you'll see with irritability.

For example, the surge of anxiety that made your child so afraid that he refused get out of the car is the same surge that makes him explode when you don't have a snack ready for him after school. Anxious kids have lots of emotions, and when anxiety goes away, the emotions don't just go away with it. They just manifest in different ways. They manifest through irritability, reactiveness, and frustration. The quick response to an anxiety-producing event is the same response kids feel when a sibling sits in their seat or when they aren't able to do the activity they had planned.

Personality

The reactive, quick-tempered behavior you see with an anxious child is often hardwired. Many parents report seeing the signs of this quick-tempered behavior when their kids were very young. Their kids were impatient about getting fed or getting their diaper changed and were hard to soothe. Especially when parents have more than one child, they notice a stark difference between their anxious child and their other kids. If this sounds like your child, it's important to recognize that some kids are more reactive than others and that reactive kids are just harder to parent.

Some kids sit in the back of the car and aren't bothered by the little things. They daydream or look out the window and don't seem affected by what's going on around them. They are much easier to parent but often are not as driven as many smart kids. The driven child can be harder to parent but often has more capacity for success, because the drive already exists within him.

The drive that makes him push to the front of the line can drive him to take advanced chemistry and study three hours a night to get an A. The drive can also make him practice soccer two hours a day until he makes the varsity team as a freshman. Drive isn't all bad; it just manifests badly when in relation to negative behavior. Because driven kids have so much intensity, they have a hard time finding ways to channel it. Finding ways to channel their intensity is imperative and is one of the most important things you can do as a parent.

Channeling the Drive

I have put a lot in this book about channeling an anxious child's energy. Many of the tools in the second section are devoted to it, and as I mentioned before, "anxiety is energy," which keeps kids awake at night and causes their minds to spin with emotion. The drive that many anxious kids possess is often seen as a negative thing when it comes to how they manage their world. Driven kids don't just exist in the world, they want to conquer it. While some kids sit back and let others win, let others slip in line in front of them, and allow other kids to have the attention, driven kids see every situation as an opportunity for them to get ahead. Mind you, this is not a choice they are making; this is just how they're wired.

When I was five years old, my eighty-year-old neighbor was having her birthday. I didn't know it until lunchtime, when my mother suggested I drop by and wish her a happy birthday. "But we don't have a present!" I shouted and was in an immediate panic to buy her a present. We lived way out in the country, and my mother was in no position to take me into town, so instead, she dug out a cross-stitched pillowcase from the back of her craft drawer and sat me down with a needle and thread and taught me how to sew. While my brother and sister laughed and played in the backyard, I sewed a pillow for my eighty-year-old neighbor for the rest of the afternoon. Just as it was getting dark, I stuffed the pillowcase with batting, and my mother sewed up the edge.

With pinpricked fingers, I delivered that pillow to my neighbor that evening, not because I was a sweet, darling child who wanted her to have a gift, but because I couldn't not do it. Once it got in my mind that my neighbor needed a present, it consumed me until it was finished. That drive has served me well over the years, but it has also worked against me. From my own experience, as well as from working with a large number of kids, I've learned that drive isn't all bad or all good. It's all about how you manage it.

With anxious kids, there is often a drive that causes major disruptions within the household. Their drive can also make them into fabulous artists, musicians, and students, because once they decide they want something, driven kids will find a way to have it. When filling out college applications someday, the driven kid will have taken five AP classes his senior year while also playing soccer and being in the school play. That drive will serve a child throughout his life, just as long as he learns how to channel it.

Staying Connected to Your Resources

Whether you're just starting the process of helping your anxious child or on the tail end of it, it's important to have an arsenal of resources to help you along the way. If you're just starting out, I would recommend that you begin reading *How to Talk so Kids will Listen and Listen so Kids will Talk* by Adele Faber and Elaine Mazlish to help you understand how to talk to your child more effectively. I also recommend you begin asking around for good therapists in your area so you'll know where to turn. Even if your child doesn't go to therapy himself, you can always go to a child therapist for parenting ideas and strategies. In parenting sessions, you can learn tailor-made strategies specific to your child's needs, apply them at home, and come back into a parenting session to discuss the outcome. You can also open up to other parents about your child's anxiety so you have a sounding board for the struggles you are having with parenting.

While it can be hard to open up about your child's struggles with anxiety, it can also be a great way for you to take care of yourself. Being open and honest about what your child is facing allows you to connect with other parents who are likely having the same issues. "My child is doing the same thing" is what many parents hear in response to the struggles they are having with their child. Parents need each other, and it's important to reach out to those who are available to you.

If your child has already gone through the process of therapy and his anxiety has greatly improved, it's still important to stay connected to the people and resources that will continue to help your child. It's not enough to terminate your relationship with the therapist and relax into the idea that things are better. Instead, stay connected, especially to your own support systems. Whether that's a supportive spouse, family member, or your own therapist, keep the momentum going by taking care of yourself. Find a support group to join, or form your own group that focuses specifically on childhood anxiety. If you have valuable information to share with other parents, reach out to them and share what you've learned. You can also meet other parents whose kids have struggled with anxiety and support each other through the bumps in the road.

It's also a good idea to maintain contact with your child's therapist so you will have a professional to call if something comes up that you don't know how to handle. You can request the school counselor check on your child from time to time and also check in with your child's teacher to make sure things are going well at school. By reading current parenting books, you can stay up to speed on childhood anxiety and learn new ideas about how to help your child. You can also expand your reading from parenting books to self-help books that will help you understand how you react to specific situations. In a nutshell, the journey of parenting an anxious child doesn't end when the anxiety goes away. It only marks a new beginning.

Part Two

Tools

Now that you have an understanding of why your smart child worries, this section will let you know what you can do to help. The tools in this section are the top parenting tools I have recommended for the past ten years. They are practical, easy to understand, and can be implemented immediately. As you read through the tools, I would encourage you to consider two things: (1) what your child needs, and (2) your current parenting style. For example, if your child is an Inward Processor, using a tool like The Five Question Rule (Tool # 4) will not be as effective, because you will be wanting your child to open up more, not less. A tool such as Naming the Anxiety (Tool #11) would be a much better option, as it would allow your child to become more vocal about his anxiety.

It is also important to consider your own limits as a parent. For example, Over Checking (Tool #10) requires a good bit of humor, and if humor is not something that comes naturally to you, the tool may seem forced. Instead, try a different tool that fits a more structured parenting style better, such as "I Did It!" List (Tool #5). Finally, I encourage you to try one tool at a time instead of trying multiple tools at once. Choose a tool you think might work well, decide on a time to implement, and make sure to implement it correctly. Often, it takes only one tool to make a difference in the life of an anxious child.

Tool #1:
Square Breathing

It's decidedly bizarre, when the "Worst Thing" happens and you find your-self still conscious, still breathing.

—Elisa Albert

Square Breathing helps kids calm down during anxious moments. It is easy to learn and can be used in any setting to de-escalate the situation.

Use When:

- *Children are in the early stages of anxiety*
- *They are "keyed up"*
- *They have a hard time relaxing*

Why the Tool Works:

1. *Breathing relaxes the body.*

   Breathing is the most important factor in remaining calm. If kids can learn to breathe slowly, their bodies will learn to relax. Yoga, meditation, and other ways of calming the body have become widely popular among adults and are now being taught to kids. Kids are now learning how to recognize tension in their bodies and relax in spite of stressful emotions. If you have access to mindfulness groups or kids' yoga in your area, they are great ways for anxious kids to learn about how their bodies feel. If you don't have that access, you can teach your child to calm himself down through breathing, without leaving your home.

2. *Counting takes the mind off the fear.*

   Half the battle is getting the breath to slow down, and the other half is getting the mind off the fear. If you have ever tried to meditate and have been flooded with thoughts, you know what I'm talking about. The mind has a way of running full speed once you try to focus on breathing. This works the same for kids. It's not enough for them to take a deep breath, let it out slowly, and then start again. Most kids have a hard time with this anyway, because they are thinking so much about their fear. They either forget to let their breath out slowly or end up holding their breath. In teaching kids how to breathe, it's important to give them something to focus on that will help take their mind off their thoughts. It's the same concept as counting sheep, an old trick for helping kids fall asleep. The belief was that if you took your mind off going to sleep, you would, in fact, go to sleep. This works very much the same when you consider breathing.

3. *Kids need a tool they can take with them anywhere.*

   I have taught many kids Square Breathing. It is the tool they deem most effective and what they resort to when they're feeling anxious both at home and at school. One parent reported looking in the rearview mirror one day to see her daughter using Square Breathing while her brother was harassing her just a seat away. Square breathing is effective because, once kids learn it, they can use it anywhere. They don't need a prop or a quiet corner to sit in. They can do Square Breathing in the car, on the school bus, in the classroom, in the bathroom, or in bed at night. Once kids learn this tool, they can rely on it getting them through anxious moments. When they are anxious about the piano recital and use Square Breathing to get through it, they will begin to believe they can get through the next piano recital. It is a tool they can use anytime, and it will help kids feel more competent.

How to Implement:

Step 1: Teach your child Square Breathing.

The steps are relatively simple and can be taught to your child in just a few minutes. Start by saying this:

"How many sides to a square? Yes, four sides. Four is a very important number, because when we do Square Breathing, we are going to count to four during every step." Now take out a pen and paper and draw a square. On each side of the box, draw the four steps. On the top left side of the box, write "In—4 counts." On the right corner, write "Hold—4 counts." On the bottom right corner, write "Out—4 counts," and on the bottom left-hand corner, write "Rest—4 counts." This process helps a child get the hang of the cycle.

Then say, "Let's start at the top left and breathe in. Let's breathe in for four counts like we're breathing in the smell of homemade chocolate chip cookies." Kids will usually smile and take a slow breath in. Count to four on your fingers for this first breath in. Then say, "Now let's hold for four seconds," while you count to four on your fingers. Now say, "Let's blow out for four counts like we're blowing on those hot cookies to cool them down." This will help your child get the sense of how to breathe out slowly. Say, "Now we're going to rest for four counts," and allow your child to take a break. Repeat the cycle three times in a row. If you stop after the first cycle, kids won't get the full benefits.

Step 2: Breathe with your child every day.

A great way to bond with your child is to breathe with him. Breathing together allows you and your child to connect around his anxiety and can be a useful tool for both of you to have. Square Breathing is best being practiced during downtimes like bedtime. Right before bed you can do Square Breathing together as a way to wind down at the end of the day. If you say, "I could use some Square Breathing. How about you?" you will get a much better response than if you say, "We have to do Square Breathing every night. Remember?" The first one allows you to join with your child. The second one places a demand on your child, and depending on his mood, he may not want to do it with you. Even if he says "no," you can do Square Breathing yourself to model how to deal with a stressful day.

Step 3: Encourage your child to do Square Breathing both inside and outside of the home.

If your child is in the middle of an anxiety attack, it's too late for Square Breathing. If he is throwing things across the room, hitting you, or rocking back and forth during a storm, you are better off trying to get your child to move rather than trying to get him to sit still and breathe. After I teach many kids to do Square Breathing, their parents tell them to do it during the middle of a huge melt-down. As one parent said, "He was holding on to my pant leg, and

I was dragging him to the kitchen, yelling, 'Square Breathe! Square Breathe!'" We laughed together when she realized the tool was completely ineffective at that point. Square Breathing takes a good bit of composure and is best used when kids are starting to spin rather than when they are in a full-blown spin. Even so, encouraging your child to do Square Breathing is a great way to help him become empowered. Before a big test say, "It might be good to do Square Breathing before the test." You can even do Square Breathing with your child the morning of the test or in the car on the way to the soccer tournament.

What You Will Find:

When you do Square Breathing yourself you will feel your body relax. When you do it with your child, you will see *his* body relax. His shoulders will go from tight to loose, and his face will go from tense to soft. Kids hold tension in their bodies, just like adults, so when it's released, they look and feel better. A tool like Square Breathing is a "one size fits all" type of tool in that it doesn't matter how young or old you are, it can be just as effective. A five-year-old can learn the tool and use it for the rest of his childhood, even the rest of his life. Once a child feels what it's like to relax their body, they will want more of it. Thus, Square Breathing can be what kids come back to over and over again.

Tool #2:
Worry Time

You can't change the past, but you can ruin the present by worrying about
the future.

—Anonymous

Worry Time is a set amount of time—fifteen minutes—when you allow your child to worry about a particular issue. When Worry Time is over, the child will have to move on.

Use When:

- *Children talk incessantly about their fears*
- *They ask you for advice but don't take it*
- *They repeat the same fears over and over again*

Why the Tool Works:

1. *The anxious mind needs a boundary.*

   The anxious mind knows no boundaries. It will spin the same thought over and over without an end in sight. The anxious mind has no sense of time either, and kids can spend days, weeks, even months worrying about something that may never happen. Sarah, an anxious ten-year-old, worried about her upcoming piano recital for three straight weeks. Her recital lasted all of five minutes, but it consumed her for more than twenty days. As adults, we can recognize this tendency. Because our minds are fully developed, we can recognize our own patterns and change them. But in the growing and developing minds of kids, being aware of their own thought patterns is extremely difficult. That's why parents need to help their kids by setting a boundary for them. When parents set boundaries, kids not only feel a sense of relief but also learn the essential skill of setting boundaries for themselves.

2. *The anxious mind needs awareness.*

The anxious mind is terribly unaware. It has no memory of past successes or recollections of when things turned out fine. Even though eight-year-old Marcus had a great soccer game last week, he can't stop worrying about not playing well this week. The anxious mind is stuck in the future, creating false stories that are not based in reality. They are based on impossible situations and worst-case scenarios and know no such thing as trust or luck or good fortune. Parents can help anxious kids become more aware by helping them stay in the moment. Instead of talking about fears whenever they come up, parents can redirect their child to a better time to talk, when both parent and children can be fully present. This helps kids become more aware of their tendency to worry excessively and allows them to put their worries to the side and enjoy the moment they are currently in.

3. *Children need to be heard.*

With the stress and schedules of daily life, it's hard to give kids the attention they need and deserve. Especially when siblings are present, kids have to fight for one-on-one attention. Take Susan, for example. She has two younger siblings and is really wanting to talk about her anxiety with her mom. Since her mom is busy trying to manage the home, Susan becomes frustrated and even more anxious, because she's not getting the outlet she needs. Anxious children need time alone with parents, especially since most anxious kids don't share their anxiety with friends or siblings. Most often, anxious kids will choose just one parent to talk to, making that parent the "go-to" parent. The "go-to" parent is usually the primary caregiver and is already busy with a hectic schedule, making it hard to be available whenever the child needs. Even though the schedule might be tight, anxious kids need time with the "go-to" parent to talk about their fears. When they don't get it, they become frustrated, and their anxiety increases.

How to Implement:

Step 1: Set aside fifteen minutes each day.

Find a time in your day when you can devote fifteen minutes solely to your child. This needs to be a time that works for both you and your child and when things are the least chaotic around the house. Good times are after dinner and before bed. Bad times are when siblings are around, when a favorite television show is on, or when friends are over. This needs to be a time when your phone is on silent and you can give your 100 percent full attention. Once you have decided on a time, begin thinking of a specific place to meet with your child. It's important to find a place where you can have a few minutes alone and where you won't be interrupted. Many parents use the few minutes before bedtime; however, if talking about worries makes your child more worried, you may want to reconsider this. You don't want your child going to bed with a spinning mind.

If that is the case, find fifteen minutes earlier in the day so your child has plenty of time to decompress before he goes to sleep.

Step 2: Tell your child about Worry Time.

Explain to your child that you are going to have a special time each day to talk about his worries. This time will be completely devoted to his worries, and you will set everything aside to listen. Say, "I really want to listen and understand; that's why I'm making a special time for us to talk." This lets your child know you care about his fears and you want to understand them. This is an especially important step if your child is an Outward Processor and you've become overwhelmed by his anxiety. Outward Processors tend to overload their parents with their anxiety, so it's important for parents to show their concern and willingness to listen. Explain that Worry Time is a time for you to listen to whatever he has to say, and if he wants advice, you will offer it. Many kids aren't looking for advice; they're looking for you to listen, and if this is the case with your child, make sure and stay in the role of listening. If you give unsolicited advice, your child will likely feel unheard. Worry Time is a time for parents to listen and reflect back what they've heard.

Step 3: Redirect worries back to Worry Time.

Even though you've set up a time to talk, kids will bring up worries outside of Worry Time. This is largely due to habit. Because anxious kids are used to expressing worries whenever they feel them, they have to learn a new habit of waiting until the right time. Having Worry Time already in place allows you to help your child develop this new habit in a sensitive way. Instead of feeling unheard, kids will feel safe knowing they'll have their special time to talk later in the day. When your child brings up a worry outside of Worry Time, simply say, "Let's talk about that at 6:00" (or whenever the designated time is). If your child seems frustrated by this, say, "I really want to hear what you have to say, but I'm not able to give my full attention right now." This lets your child know you really care about his fears and you want to be able to devote your full attention. At 6:00, when you meet for Worry Time, say, "I really appreciate you waiting to share your worries. I really care about what you have to say and am ready to listen." This rewards patience in your child, and patience is something every anxious child needs more of.

What You Will Find:

The anxious mind is not used to redirecting thoughts. It's used to processing thoughts at rapid speeds and then going into neutral. Therefore, when kids worry, it's intense, but then it goes away. In fact, when kids are given a chance to talk during Worry Time, they often say, "I don't need to talk about that anymore." Therefore, you likely won't need the fifteen minutes you set aside for Worry Time. You should still set aside that time, but the reality is that worries come and go. At 4:00, they may be intense, but at 6:00, they are nonexistent. If your child sits down and says she's not worried anymore, point this out. Say, "You really seemed worried two hours ago. That's interesting how you're not worried about that anymore. I guess some worries just come and go." By saying this, you help your child realize that what was a huge fear two hours ago has faded away to nothing at all.

Tool #3:
Changing the Channel

Problems can't be solved at the same level of awareness that created them.

—Albert Einstein

Changing the Channel is a way for kids to change their thoughts from negative to positive. Using the example of a television set, anxious kids can learn how to change their thinking quickly and effectively.

Use When:

- *Children are stuck in a negative place*
- *They aren't thinking rationally*
- *Talking doesn't seem to help*

Why the Tool Works:

1. *The anxious mind gets stuck.*

   Anxious kids get thoughts and ideas stuck in their mind. It may be a worry they can't seem to get past or an idea they can't seem to get over, but regardless, anxious kids have a hard time moving on. This is partly due to anxiety surges and partly due to their emotional intensity. Anxious kids feel things deeply and intensely, and to expect them to regroup on their own is often too much to ask. Their fears are so big that they overtake their minds and everything else gets put on the back burner. Eleven-year-old Daniel became consumed with his sister getting a computer and him not getting one. He just wouldn't let it go and kept bringing it up every opportunity he had. His parents used Changing the Channel to get him to focus on playing his drum set, something he enjoyed much more than playing on the computer, and he was able to move on.

Being stuck is also why you hear kids say "I don't care" when you threaten to take something away. Their emotional energy is so big that in that moment, it doesn't matter if they have no privileges at all. They are stuck in a negative emotional state that trumps everything else. That's why Changing the Channel works so well. It allows kids the space to get unstuck.

2. *It removes blame and punishment (for the time being).*

Consequences can get out of hand. When children are stuck in a negative place, parents are desperate to find something to get them out of it. If taking away dessert doesn't work, then you take away tomorrow's play date, and before long, you've taken away a week's worth of privileges only to realize you've gone overboard and give it all back again. It's important to remember that the only point to giving consequences is so children will do something different the next time. If a child comes out of time-out making the same choice that got him in it, the time-out was ineffective. That's why punishing kids while they're emotionally spinning doesn't work. When they're angry, they're irrational and don't have the capacity to see their wrong actions, so they don't learn anything from consequences. Changing the Channel delays consequences long enough for kids to gain per-spective. It doesn't mean kids won't receive a consequence; it just means you'll address the incident when your child is calm enough to process their actions, and you're calm enough to give appropriate consequences.

3. *It gives kids a chance to regroup.*

Kids say and do things they don't mean. When they get upset, they dig themselves into holes they can't figure out how to get out of. They say they hate you, hate themselves, and that they wish they were never born. They hit, kick, and destroy things, only to feel terrible about it later and apologize. Changing the Channel is a great way to throw a rope and rescue kids before they get in too deep. When the tool works effectively, kids will grab the rope and allow themselves to be pulled out of a negative place. They'll let things go, make a good choice, and turn things around. The negative cycle will be broken, and anxious kids will be on stable ground again.

How to Implement:

Step 1: Change the focus.

Just as you'd change the channel on a television set, you can change the thought process for your child. If you are able to take your child in a different direction, you will see your child shift from negative emotions to positive emotions or, at the very least, neutral emotions. There are several ways to do this:

- **Random Statements**—When your child is emotionally spinning, you can say, "Guess who I saw today?" This will throw your child off track long enough to wonder who you saw. The space of wondering creates an emotional release for your child.
- **Common Interests**—"I wonder who the Cardinals are playing

tonight?" is a statement that will cause your child to stop and think, thus removing the focus from what he was upset about.

- **Exciting News**—If you have something exciting to tell your child, wait until they need a good boost to deliver it. If you just firmed up your vacation plans to Florida, tell your child at a time when they need something else to focus on.

Step 2: Try to get them on board.

Sometimes just changing the direction of the conversation works. Other times, you'll have to dig for some interest. If kids are really stuck, they may not bite, and if that's the case, move on to something else. Say "I thought you would be interested in the Cardinals game tonight. I guess not" and move on. Don't just move on to another topic, but move on emotionally. Emotionally detach from your child's intense emotions while he's in a negative state. If you go to the level of where your child is, you will only make the situation worse.

Another approach is to explain Changing the Channel to your child and encourage him to use the tool on his own. For example, when your child is upset, you can say, "I see you're angry. How about Changing the Channel?" This acknowledges your child's feelings and gives him an idea of what will help him through it. If he's still in a rational place, he'll be able to change the direction of his emotions and move on to something else.

Step 3: Address the incident later.

If your child's actions warrant a punishment, come back and address the issue later. Once both you and your child have calmed down, say, "What you did today was not okay." You don't need to ask your child why he acted in such a way (as this only promotes lying) but instead, ask what he could have done differently. If a punishment is necessary, go ahead and give it now. Make sure you've come up with an appropriate consequence and that you're not still upset about the event. If possible, try to make the punishment fit the crime. For example, if your child broke something, he needs to use his allowance to pay for it, or if he said mean things to his sibling, he needs to do something nice for her. For this last step, timing is everything. Make sure your child has enough time to regain composure but not so long he's forgotten what happened. A general rule of thumb is to discuss consequences during the same day the actions were committed. If you wait until the next day, the child may have forgotten what happened.

What You Will Find:

Kids need help getting out of a negative place. Telling them things like "Try taking three deep breaths" and "You should be grateful we're even going to the mall" while they're upset is not helpful. When kids are upset, they're not thinking rationally, and these kinds of comments only make things worse. Instead, change the conversation to something outside of the emotional event. This provides just enough space for kids to breathe and collect themselves. They may come back to the distressing event, but this time they will have less emotional intensity. They'll be able to think more rationally or realize they aren't really that upset after all. The longer kids sit in negative emotions, the harder it is for them to move on, but when you break up the emotional cycle, things will settle down much more quickly.

Tool #4:
The Five Question Rule

Anxiety is a thin stream of fear trickling through the mind. If encouraged, it cuts a channel into which all other thoughts are drained.

—Arthur Somers Roche

The Five Question Rule allows kids to ask only five questions about the same worry within one day. They can choose what questions they ask and when, just as long as they don't go over five.

Use When:

- *Children are asking repetitive questions*
- *They aren't really listening to your answers*
- *Your child's anxiety isn't lessening*

Why the Tool Works:

1. *Asking repetitive questions isn't good for kids.*

   Anxious kids ask repetitive questions without any awareness. "What time are we leaving?" an anxious kid will ask twenty times in the space of an hour. Even when you say "At 1:00," they will keep asking even though you've given a clear answer. Their questions are rooted in anxiety; therefore, the answer you give doesn't really matter. Even if you changed your answer to "We're leaving at 2:00," it wouldn't make much difference to an anxious child. Asking the question is what relieves their anxiety, not hearing the answer. After hearing the answer, a child feels a few moments of relief, but their anxiety comes right back again. That's why setting boundaries around repetitive questions is so important. Setting boundaries around a child's questions decreases anxiety rather than increasing it.

2. *Anxious kids need to learn to self-soothe.*

   Self-soothing does not come naturally to kids. Kids want their parents to solve problems for them, protect them from danger, and make sure nothing bad happens to them. As kids get older, they have to learn to solve problems on their own, and doing this is tough for anxious kids, especially during times of high anxiety. However, once anxious kids develop the ability to self-soothe, they will be better able to handle things on their own. When they're having problems with friends, they'll be able to find a new group. When they don't win the race, they'll be able to keep their composure and congratulate the other team. These skills are imperative for kids to grow up and lead healthy lives. By learning to solve their own problems, anxious kids learn how to self-soothe, thus learning how to function in a world where things will not always go their way.

3. *Communication needs a boundary.*

   Even though you want your child to feel like he can tell you anything, when he's already told you something thirty times, telling you again is no longer effective. Your response is not going to change, and his telling you again is only going to make him more anxious. That's why continuing to talk about things doesn't make anxious kids feel better; it actually makes them feel worse. When they are in a rational place, they can find ways to help themselves and actually listen to what you have to say.

When they are irrational, they are not able to solve problems or take in what you have to say. That's why parents need to set boundaries around communication. Saying, "You've already asked that question eleven times. I'm not going to answer it again," helps anxious kids become more aware. Choosing not to answer the question also sets a boundary around your child's anxiety. The above response helps anxious kids understand just how much they've been saying something and just how little it has changed anything in the big picture.

How to Implement:

Step 1: Limit your child to five questions.

The Five Question Rule is used when kids ask the same question repeatedly, or when they ask multiple anxiety-related questions. These questions generally occur before anxiety-producing events and are aimed at releasing anxiety and/or getting out of having to do something. For example, Madeline is worried about going to a sleepover on Saturday because they watched a scary movie at her last sleepover. Whenever her anxious thoughts begin, she will start asking questions: "What if they watch a scary movie? What should I do? Should I even go? Can I call you? What if they watch a scary movie?" If she starts worrying on Wednesday, she will ask the questions for the next four days, generally asking more and more as the sleepover gets closer. As a parent, it's important to implement the Five Question Rule at the beginning of a question cycle. In Madeline's case, if she has already asked twenty questions and then you implement the tool, it will be less effective than if you implemented the tool when her questions were starting. When your child begins asking questions about specific events, simply say, "You've already asked that question three times. I will answer that question only two more times. You can decide when you want to use your other two questions." This allows anxious kids to stop and think before they ask the next question. If their question is not that pressing, they will hold it until they feel more compelled to ask.

Step 2: Keep track of the questions and/or time.

Pay attention to how many questions your child is asking and in what time frame. If you look at the clock and realize your child has asked the same question twelve times in thirty minutes, point this out by saying, "You know, Charlie. You've asked that same question twelve times in the past thirty minutes. You must be really worried about that." Charlie has no idea how many times he's asked the question or why he has started asking it so often within the last thirty minutes. When you make him aware, he begins to understand how worried he really is and how unproductive asking the questions have been. Keeping track of questions also helps you as a parent. In the middle of a busy day, it's hard to keep track of just how much your child is asking of you. By keeping track, you can begin to see how excessive it is and feel more empowered to set boundaries. Where you used to say, "Yes, we still have to go to the dentist," twenty times, now you are limiting your child's questions.

Step 3: Take time to answer the five questions your child does ask.

This is important. If you are going to limit your child to five questions, make sure you stop and think about your five responses before just giving a short "yes" or "no" answer. If you simply say, "Yes, we still have to go" or "No, you can't stay home," you really aren't getting to the heart of the question. The heart of the question is based in fear; therefore, to address what your child's concerns really are, you must target that emotion. A more effective response is "You really seem worried about going to the doctor. I know you don't want to go, but I'm sorry, we have to." By targeting the feeling underneath the question, you are connecting with your child while also shedding light into his own anxiety. Because most kids are unaware of why they are asking questions in the first place, when you acknowledge their feeling, you help them process their own anxiety rather than keeping the conversation on the surface with "yes" and "no" answers.

What You Will Find:

When you set boundaries, anxious kids will learn to handle their emotions in healthier ways. They will catch themselves asking incessant questions and stop themselves when they've already received an answer. They will also learn to be less reactive to their own anxiety and to rely on their own coping skills instead of you. If they know you won't continue answering their questions, they will figure out ways to feel better on their own. They will learn how to self-soothe and also how to move on to something else, because you are no longer being the source in which their anxiety manifests.

Tool #5:
"I Did It!" List

If you see ten troubles coming down the road, you can be sure that nine will run into the ditch before they reach you.

—Calvin Coolidge

"I Did It!" List is a record of successes that helps anxious kids build confidence in their ability to overcome difficult things. After each success, they write down what they accomplished and what tool they used, so they can draw from their past experiences.

Use When:

- *Children are low on confidence*
- *They have a hard time remembering past successes*
- *They have just achieved something great*

Why the Tool Works:

1. *The anxious mind doesn't remember the good.*
   Anxiety casts a shadow of negativity on the lives of kids, making things seem overwhelming and impossible. It's not that anxious kids haven't overcome great obstacles in the past; it's just that their anxious minds can't recall them. The anxious mind remembers only the fears, the times things didn't go well, the pain of past failures. Even when you remind anxious kids of a recent accomplishment, they will say, "This is different! This is worse!"

Not because that's really what they believe, but because during an anxious moment, that's all they can see. That's why keeping a record of brave moments as anxious kids experience them is so important. Keeping a written record allows them to see their accomplishments rather than just remembering them. They can look at a concrete list of the difficult things they've overcome and realize they are much more capable than they feel at the moment.

2. *Kids are more capable than they think they are.*

When kids make an effort, they can tackle almost anything. Just the willingness to show up is often all it takes to get an anxious child from Point A to Point B. Getting to Point A poses the biggest problem, not the journey to Point B. Anxiety is what stops kids from trying to do something difficult. It kicks in before kids even get to Point A, locking them down and making them feel unable to make the journey. For example, if your child is afraid of swim lessons, getting him there is the hardest part. Once he's there and realizes it's not that bad, he'll settle in and may even like it. If he doesn't like it, his survival skills will likely kick in and allow him to complete the lesson anyway. It's never as bad as kids think it's going to be, and showing up to make an effort is the only way for anxious kids to realize this. "I had fun!" is what many parents hear after they have made their child do something. Knowing they had a good time makes the struggle to get them there seem worth it.

3. *Success builds confidence.*

Once kids start facing their fears and overcoming them, an amazing thing happens: they want to try more difficult things. An eight-year-old boy I was working with said recently, "I'm not afraid of monsters anymore. I'm going upstairs on my own now too. And guess what I'm doing this weekend? Going to my first sleepover!" After he came back from the sleepover, he said, "I did it! And I wasn't even scared!" The taste of success allowed him to participate in something he had been avoiding. When kids start doing things they were afraid of in the past, they build the momentum it takes to help them do even greater things.

How to Implement:

Step 1: Make an "I Did It!" List.

The best time to start an "I Did It!" List is right after your child has achieved something great. While he's still feeling positive and proud of himself, say, "You have accomplished so many great things. Let's keep track of them so we both don't forget how well you've done." Then, using colorful paper, posterboard, or a handmade book, allow your child make a list of his accomplishments. Using glitter, special markers, etc., write "I Did It!" List on the front cover or top of the paper. It's best if your child writes the words himself, as seeing his own writing will be more meaningful than seeing yours. If your child doesn't like to write, you can write for him just so long as the activity is enjoyable and not laborsome. Some kids will want to tape their list to their bedroom wall, and others will want to hide it away so it doesn't get ruined. Allow your child the freedom to place his list wherever he likes, just as long as he can account for it when it's time to add something new.

Step 2: Record successes, including the date.

Begin recording your child's most recent successes (including the date) and work backwards. For example, if your child just completed a piano recital, write: *Piano Recital—10/11/12*. This allows him to record the name of the success as well as remember the date. He can also add Square Breathing to remind him of the tool that helped him through it. After he's written his most recent successes, add to them by asking your child what he's most proud of. Start first with the fears he was able to overcome, and then move on to other things, such as awards, achievements, etc. The more successes your child can recall on his own, the better. If he has trouble recalling successes on his own, remind him of the difficult situations he's faced and how he was able to overcome them. Recalling even the smallest successes is important when you start out. Try to have between three to five successes written down before you finish the activity, and then put the list in a safe place.

Step 3: Add successes as they occur.

As your child overcomes difficult situations, have him write them down. Bring out the "I Did It!" List as soon as you get home so your child can record his success. When he doesn't remember to do it on his own, remind him so he won't forget his accomplishment. If he just finished the piano recital, say "You did so well! I really want you to remember this" to encourage your child to take the time to add it to his list. While he's still dressed up and in the mood he can add his accomplishment and feel the immediate relief of overcoming his fear. You can even use the "I Did It!" List to motivate your child to have the courage to do something difficult. By saying "I really hope you can do this. I think it would be great to add to your list," he can imagine what it will feel like once he overcomes the difficult situation. He can visualize himself writing the success on his list, and that often provides enough incentive to carry him through.

What You Will Find:

Having a list of successes helps raise self-esteem in anxious kids. Looking back at what they've accomplished, anxious kids will start to feel better about their ability to cope. They will begin to see themselves as capable instead of debilitated and see their current situation as a challenge instead of a roadblock. As successes are added to their list, they'll become motivated to add even harder things and take pride in handling situations they originally thought were impossible. Many kids keep their "I Did It!" List for years. They keep adding to it to see how many hard things they can overcome. They can look back and remember how much they struggled with something and how trivial it seems now. They will realize that going to sleepaway camp wasn't that big of a deal and that a problem with a friend ended up being nothing at all. Having a record of conquered anxieties helps kids gain perspective and not react so strongly to new situations.

Tool #6:
The Marble System

The best way to make children good is to make them happy.

—*Oscar Wilde*

The Marble System is a reward system where kids are asked to do three daily tasks, receiving a marble for each one. At the end of the day, the child can get a reward for completing the tasks. The Marble System is a fast, effective way to change the dynamic in the home from negative to positive.

Use When:

- *Children are disruptive*
- *They are seeking negative attention*
- *They are resistant to doing daily tasks*

Why the Tool Works:

1. *Kids want to do well.*

   Kids don't want to get in trouble. What they really want is to do well. They want to be accepted, loved, and appreciated, but when they can't figure out how to get what they want, they fall into negative patterns. Negative patterns are where disruptive behavior is born. Once kids fall into a pattern of acting out, not brushing their teeth, not listening to what has been said, they begin getting negative attention; and negative attention is addictive. When kids get in trouble, all eyes are on them, and while disrupting may not feel good, it feels much better than receiving no attention at all. This is why it's so hard to break negative behavior patterns. When kids find something that gives them the attention they want, they keep doing it until they find something else that works. When they are stuck in negative behavior, you have to find something that gives them more attention than the attention they are receiving for making poor choices.

2. *Kids desire positive attention.*

Positive attention allows kids to be praised for doing the right thing. When you give a child positive attention, you are saying *I appreciate you making the right choice.* This can happen in a variety of ways, but to be most effective, positive attention needs to be delivered in a way that matters to your child. If your child craves one-on-one attention, their positive attention will be time with you. If they love computer games or sweets, you'll reward them with extra computer time or an extra scoop of ice cream. Regardless of what the reward is, kids respond better to positive attention than they do negative attention. When you point out the positive, kids see themselves as capable of doing well and are encouraged to repeat the positive behavior again. When you point out the negative, kids feel frustrated and are more likely to repeat the negative behavior out of frustration than they are to change it. While you need to address negative behavior at times, focusing on what went right versus what went wrong is a much better approach.

3. *Changing the dynamic works.*

When kids are disruptive, a negative dynamic is created in the home. There is an atmosphere of frustration and resistance, and parents spend inordinate amounts of time trying to get their kids to do simple tasks. It may start out with teeth brushing, then it turns into taking plates to the sink and picking up clothes. While these are relatively minor tasks, they can turn into major events. A two-minute task can turn into a twenty-minute meltdown, and the rest of the night will be thrown off. The Marble System changes this dynamic by rewarding kids for doing the right thing instead of punishing them for doing the wrong thing. Instead of having to ask five times for your child to brush his teeth, your child now *wants* to brush his teeth, because now he's being rewarded for it.

How to Implement:

Step 1: Set up the Marble System.

Buy a small, clear jar for each of your children. It is best if all of your children participate in the Marble System, not just the child who's causing the disruption. Then, buy a bag of marbles, enough for each of your children to be able to put ten-plus marbles inside their jar. Now, choose three tasks you would like your children to do each day. The tasks need to be concrete and measurable, so there can be no argument about whether they were performed. For example, "brushing teeth" is a concrete task, whereas "being nice" is not. "Being nice" is too vague and provides an opening for an argument, so it will not be effective. The tasks can be the same or different for each child, just as long as each child is assigned one easy task, one moderate task, and one difficult task. This allows your child to have immediate success rather than feeling a sense of failure, as well as being challenged. Talk with your spouse about the tasks and agree to be on the same page. Consistency is crucial to the Marble System being effective.

Step 2: Introduce it to your kids.

Introduce the Marble System when things are going well. When your kids are in a positive place and everyone is getting along, explain that you are starting a new reward system. It's important to show your enthusiasm during this time and to refrain from saying anything negative about their past behavior. This should be a time of excitement, not of blaming or judging. Using poster board (or something similar), explain the three daily tasks each child needs to do to receive a marble. Be specific, and make sure each child fully understands what is expected of them. Then give a start date within three days of when you explain the system, so your kids don't lose momentum. On the start date, show lots of enthusiasm, and after each task is done, allow each child to place one marble in the jar on their own (this empowers children and removes you from being the middleman). If your child shows resistance, encourage him by saying "I really want you to get a marble for brushing your teeth" instead of saying "If you don't brush your teeth, you won't get a marble." At the end of each day, your kids can either cash in their marbles for a daily treat (such as extra computer time) or they can save their marbles for something larger. When and how they cash in their marbles is not as important as investing in the process.

Step 3: Make adjustments.

You may need to adjust the tasks, time of day, or the rewards your children receive after implementing the Marble System. You may also find that when the novelty wears off, kids may need more incentive to complete their tasks. If they are angry, they might say, "I don't care if I get a marble," and on busy days, they may even forget to do their tasks. A great way to rebuild the momentum is to give out extra marbles randomly for good behavior. Without giving your kids any advance notice, reward them for doing the right thing. For example, if one child hits another while in the car, when you walk in the door, reward the child who got hit for not hitting back. When you walk in the house, say, "I'm giving you an extra marble, Adam. I'm very proud of you for not hitting in the car." You don't want to add "even though your brother hit you," as this will likely make your other child angry. Suddenly, the child who got hit has an extra marble for doing the right thing. You can also use extra marbles as an incentive for doing the right thing during difficult times (such as car trips, doctor's appointments, etc.). Before leaving, you can say, "If you sit quietly in the waiting room, you will get an extra marble." This is especially useful when kids are saving up their marbles for something big.

What You Will Find:

Just as getting in trouble is addictive, doing the right thing is addictive too. When kids start making the right choices, they end up making the wrong choices less and less. Once the dynamic has shifted, kids will gain enough momentum to make positive changes in all areas of their lives. The Marble System is also a great way for parents to get everyone on the same page. Once your kids are doing the right thing, you can get a better idea of what is going on with your anxious child. You can get a better sense of his anxiety and how his siblings are feeding into it. When there is chaos, this is not possible. When the Marble System is in place and things are running smoothly, you can address the issues you weren't able to address before.

Tool #7:
Giving Your Child a Role

Worry gives a small thing a big shadow.

—Swedish Proverb

Giving Your Child a Role helps kids feel more comfortable at social events. The roles are fun (such as handing out cupcakes at a party) and allow anxious kids to settle more easily into social situations.

Use When:

- *Children are worried about a specific event*
- *They struggle in social situations*
- *They have a hard time sharing attention*

Why the Tool Works:

1. *The anxious mind fears the unknown.*

   For anxious kids, there's nothing worse than not knowing what to expect. Not knowing who's going to be at the party, whom they're going to sit by, or how they're going to fit into a group situation causes anxiety to skyrocket, especially for kids with Relational Anxiety. When kids don't know what to expect, they create stories about situations. As a way to prepare themselves for the event, they come up with worst-case scenarios and begin to believe them. Once they buy into a belief that things won't go well, they are hard to convince otherwise. That's why giving them a role works so well. Instead of creating a negative story, you give them a positive story they can begin playing in their mind.

2. *Having a role eases the pressure of social situations.*

When kids have a role, they know where they fit into a situation. If they are the ones who pass out the cupcakes at a party, they'll have something to look forward to. Passing out cupcakes is a great example of a role every child wants to have. Because all kids love cupcakes, the person who passes them out is going to be a popular person at the party. Instead of slinking down against a back wall, your child can now stand at the front of the party with a job. If you know your child's role beforehand, make sure and tell him, as it will ease the pressure of new social situations. It will also help him feel excited about going to the event, and when kids are excited, they smile and have a much easier time making friends.

3. *Kids will rise to the expectation that is set for them.*

When you set high expectations for kids, they will respond. Six-year-old Matthew was anxious about going to a new school, but his teacher made him a line leader that day. Matthew jumped in the car after the first day of school, saying, "I got to be the line leader on my first day!" The role helped him ease into what would have been a very hard day for him. That's why kids love to help; they want to be chosen to do something important. When kids have an important role, they will rise to the expectation of their role and want to do it as well as possible. Even if their role is simply passing out cupcakes, they will not only enjoy the event more but also see themselves as capable in social situations. Being in front of other people also helps kids perform better. When they can be a leader, they will automatically feel important and full of confidence. This confidence can also be seen when they are chosen to play a role at a social event. Even if your child's role seems minor, making a big deal out of it will help your child feel a burst of confidence because he was chosen to do it.

How to Implement:

Step 1: Choose a role for your child.

If you are throwing the party, you'll have plenty of roles to choose from. If you are attending an event, you may have a harder time coming up with a role. What's important is to think creatively about what role your child can play. If it's an event you're hosting, ask your child to hand out or hold something everyone is interested in (like cupcakes). If it's not your event and you have a close relationship with the host, ask if your child can help out in some way. If you have no control at all (first soccer practice, dance lesson, etc.) give your child the role of giving something away. Give him an extra bottle of Gatorade or an extra stick of gum he can hand to someone while he's there. Allowing kids to give something away is a great way to make friends. This also helps kids shift their focus from thinking about who they're going to talk to, to finding someone they can share with.

Step 2: Invest in the role.

It's important to be excited about your child's role. If it's handing out cupcakes, talk about the cupcakes and how everyone will be excited to receive them. If it's the extra bottle of Gatorade, talk about how happy the other child will be in receiving a bottle of Gatorade on a hot day. Helping your child see himself in that role will help relieve the pressure of the social situation and allow your child to become more relaxed. Kids who are relaxed attract friends because they exude confidence. Giving your child a role will help him exude the same amount of confidence, so he knows where he fits in a given situation. Especially if it's a situation where he will not be the center of attention (a sibling's birthday party), help him realize that while it's not his birthday, he will still play an important role at the party.

Step 3: Be there to help along the way.

If your child begins acting in ways that aren't conducive to playing the role, dangle a carrot. Say, "I really want you to be able to hand out cupcakes, but from the way you're acting, it doesn't look like you'll be able to. Please show me you can handle this." This will help your child remember the role he was excited to play and give him incentive to improve his behavior. If your child is shy about the role, be there to encourage him. Give him ideas about how to make the role more comfortable, and be there to walk alongside him while he's in the role. You can stand beside him at the beginning of the party and help him get started so he'll be able to accomplish the task.

What You Will Find:

Anxious kids find relief in having a role. Instead of worrying about how situations will unfold, they'll be excited about the role they will be playing. They will also begin to see social situations differently. After having several social situations go well, they will be more confident that social situation will go well in the future. They will find themselves more open to letting social situations play out and

will learn that they are able to cope just fine. It's all about momentum, and when anxious kids are able to gain momentum, they will
become more comfortable in situations that used to terrify them.

Tool #8:
Structuring the Unstructured

Blessed is the person who is too busy to worry in the daytime and too sleepy to worry at night.

—Anonymous

Structuring the Unstructured puts boundaries around unstructured time so kids don't become more worried. It is a great tool to use during breaks from school, weekends, or after-school times.

Use When:

- *Children don't adjust well to change*
- *They like structure and routine*
- *They are in a period of downtime*

Why the Tool Works:

1. *The anxious mind likes routine.*

   Day after day, anxious kids do the same thing. They get up at a certain time, eat a certain kind of cereal, get dropped off at school, learn the same subjects in the same order, then get picked up at the same time, eat dinner, brush their teeth, and go to bed, only to do it all over again. Then summer hits…and everything changes. Then suddenly, there are no set bedtimes or wake-up times. Instead of a busy school day, there are hours of unstructured time, and anxious kids become flooded by thoughts: What am I going to do today? What should I do today? What's happening next? When will I see my friends? Will I even have any friends when school starts back again? These thoughts occur not only once school lets out, but also often weeks, even months, before school ends. They also occur during fall and winter breaks from school and at the end of a school day when there are no activities planned.

2. *Structure helps ease the anxious mind.*

    When anxious kids have structure, their minds relax. Instead of wondering what's going to happen next, they *know* what's going to happen next. Instead of wondering what to do, who to play with, or how to spend their day, they can relax into a schedule that's already made out for them. For 180 days each year, kids get this type of structure. That's why breaks from school are so hard. The abrupt change in structured vs. unstructured time is too drastic, and instead of adjusting slowly, anxious kids panic. Structure also helps the weekends and after-school times go more smoothly. Because anxious kids do better with structure, having a schedule in place allows them to know what's coming. They will know what activities lay ahead and will be able to settle into a routine more smoothly.

3. *Kids need a balance between structured and unstructured time.*

    When kids become too structured, there is no room for creativity and play. When they become too unstructured, they become out of control and anxious. The key is balancing the two. By including unstructured time within the structure of a day, kids can experience the benefits of unstructured time without the anxiety of worrying about how long it's going to last. Within an eight-hour day, kids can have an hour or two of unstructured time. This allows them time for creativity and play, while they can also relax in knowing the unstructured time will have an ending. Having small amounts of unstructured time still allows kids to foster creativity and independence, but they do not become anxious and overwhelmed. Once anxious kids get used to having unstructured time, the time slots can be extended to several hours or even a full day.

How to Implement:

Step 1: Make a schedule ahead of time.

Using a large calendar that has enough space to write a number of activities within each day, begin scheduling unstructured time. You can buy a large white calendar or make your own, but the point here is to: (1) have enough room for activities to be written, and (2) make it visible enough for your kids to see it at any given time. For example, if you are scheduling the summer, begin your calendar with the last day of school and schedule until the day before school starts the next year. Start by blocking out vacations, sleepaway camps, day camps, time with grandparents, etc., then fill in the holes. On the days your child is at camp, you won't have to structure the evenings as much, as he'll likely be worn out. On the days where he's not, schedule play dates, picnics, bike rides, etc. You can either schedule half-day activities or full-day activities. The in-between activities are where the unstructured time comes in.

Step 2: Ask for your child's input.

You may have ideas for your child's summer, and he may have ideas of his own. The important part is to give anxious kids a sense of what is going to happen. If you are sending your child to sleepaway camp and you don't plan on telling him until a week before, you're going to have some problems making your calendar. It's better to give anxious kids an idea of what to expect. That way, if there is a part of the summer your anxious child is dreading, you can put the things he really enjoys on both sides of the event. You can put his favorite summer camp right before he starts the dreaded swim team and a family vacation right after. When he looks at the calendar, he will be able to see the whole picture rather than just worrying about the one part of the summer he is dreading.

Step 3: Stick to the schedule.

When in doubt, stick to the schedule. If your child does/does not want to do an activity and you end up making last-minute adjustments, you will give your child the sense that the schedule can't be trusted. Even if it's something exciting, changing the schedule can cause chaos, unless there is an empty spot where the new activity can easily fit. Especially if the event is something your child is dreading, changing the schedule to reduce anxiety only exacerbates it at a later date. The easiest way to handle these situations is: If you've already made plans, stick to them. Even if you schedule something your child doesn't like, stick with the plan anyway. Help your child get through the anxiety-producing event without letting him out of it completely.

What You Will Find:

Kids will handle unstructured time much better if there is a schedule in place. When kids know what to expect, unstructured time doesn't feel so overwhelming. If they know they are going on a picnic at 12:00, what happens before and after 12:00 is not as important to them. Until 12:00 they can play independently and enjoy the morning, knowing the unstructured time will end soon. After the picnic, they'll be more tired than they were in the morning and can settle into unstructured time much easier. Over time, anxious kids will get more comfortable with unstructured time. They'll not only get used to it, but will also learn to enjoy the time they have to be creative, independent, and free from activities. Many anxious kids actually end up craving unstructured time. They will go from despising it to wanting more of it, because once they settle in, they realize it can actually be a lot of fun.

Tool #9:
Blanket Tool

Where everything is bad it must be good to know the worst.

—*Francis Bradley*

Blanket Tool helps kids get out of black-and-white thinking by helping them see the gray. The tool dissects situations so kids can see that both good and bad happen within any given day.

Use When:

- *Children are in black/white thinking*
- *They have a hard time seeing the good*
- *They are resistant to thinking differently*

Why the Tool Works:

1. *The anxious mind clings to negative events.*
   The birthday party went perfectly...except for one thing. Just when he went to take a sip of Kool-Aid, someone ran into him, and the Kool-Aid spilled all over his shirt. To an anxious kid, this will ruin the whole party. When he climbs in the car and shouts, "The party was awful!" his parent might assume that a number of things went wrong when, in reality, the majority of things went right. After the party, an anxious kid will see only the Kool-Aid incident. Everything else will be blocked out by a cloud of embarrassment. As a parent, it's hard to hear that

"everything was awful." Many times you are at the same party as your child, and you see him laughing and having fun, only for him to tell you later how miserable he was. It's important to remember that children are concrete thinkers, so they see things as black/white. The Blanket Tool allows them to see the gray.

2. *Negative events overshadow positive events.*

When negative things happen to anxious kids, the positive gets lost. This is partly because kids' minds aren't fully developed, and they don't have the perspective of adults. It's also because the amygdala is grouping together "bad" things and causing kids to be more hypervigilant than they need to be. The other part is that kids want you to know how bad they feel. If an anxious kid gets in the car and says, "The party went great except that Kool-Aid was spilled on my shirt," it totally devalues the Kool-Aid incident, which was devastating. So instead, an anxious child will talk only about the Kool-Aid incident instead of all of the good things that happened. In his mind, the Kool-Aid incident is all he can see, so there's no use in talking about anything else. Until he feels better about the situation, that is all he will want to talk about.

3. *When kids see both the good and the bad, they gain perspective.*

Anxious kids are capable of seeing both the good and bad, but they're going to need some help. Without the help of a parent, anxious kids will see all birthday parties as bad or the person who ran into them as bad or themselves as bad for spilling the Kool-Aid in the first place. But when you start picking apart the event, anxious kids will begin to see that good things happened both before and after the Kool-Aid incident. They will see that all parties aren't bad, that the kid who ran into them really is nice, and that this is the only party where such an incident has happened. Anxious kids will be able to see this if the situation is addressed at the right time. When they are open, they will be able to see that there are gray areas in which both good and bad things can happen. When children are able to recognize this, real growth takes place.

How to Implement:

Step 1: Listen carefully to what's being said.

Before you try and change your child's perspective, make sure and listen to what's being said. When your child first jumps in the car, I recommend that for the first ten minutes, you just let him vent. Don't disagree or try to help him see things differently. Instead, just listen and empathize. Express that you are sorry this terrible thing happened and you understand how he feels. After he's calmed down, start processing the whole event rather than just the one thing that went wrong. When you allow your child to vent, you allow him to get to a more rational place. When his mind is spinning, there's no sense trying to rationalize; he won't hear you anyway. So just be patient and allow the process to work organically once your child has calmed down long enough to let what you are saying soak in.

Step 2: Tease apart the day.

Start with the moment your child walked into the party. Say, "So when you first got there, what happened?" Then say, "What happened next?" Don't try to point out the positive yet, just listen and see what your child experienced. Take your child back through the party, step-by-step, so you can get a better idea of what happened. This process helps kids go back in their minds and recall what happened. Since they have blocked out every other event except for the anxious one, this takes them back through the events as they happened. Often during this "teasing out" period, their mood state will change. They will remember something funny or exciting and begin telling you about it, all the while forgetting about the distressing event. They will tell you what someone said or how much fun a game was. Overall, they will begin to see that good things happened too.

Step 3: Put it back together again.

During the "teasing out" phase, if your child lets go of the anxious event and begins to see that the party wasn't all bad, your job is done. If he doesn't, help him discover a new way of thinking about the event. Say, "It sounds like you had a pretty good time, all except for…" If your child agrees with this statement, that's great. If he resists it, let it go. By resisting, he is telling you he's not ready to gain a new perspective. If kids aren't ready, no matter what you say, it's not going to change anything. Wait until he's moved on and say, "That game at the party really sounded fun. Can you tell me more about it?" This gives your child another opportunity to tell you about the good. If he is willing to tell you about it, say, "I'm glad you got to have some fun at that party after all," and let it go. You will have plenty of chances to help your child see the good.

What You Will Find:

When kids are able to see that negative experiences and positive experiences can coexist, they begin to change the way they see things.

They widen their perspective and become more open to anxiety-producing events because they feel like good things can come from them. When kids are experiencing high amounts of anxiety, they may not be able to gain perspective, but later, after they have calmed down, they can see the good instead of just seeing the bad. Seeing both the good and bad within a given situation is a higher-level thinking skill anxious kids can learn. If kids are able to recall events as not all bad, they will be less likely to be afraid of them in the future and more likely to be open to taking more risks.

Tool #10:
Over Checking

That the birds of worry fly over your head, this you cannot change, but that they build nests in your hair, this you can prevent.

—*Chinese Proverb*

Over Checking is a reverse psychology technique that throws kids off guard. It changes the dynamic from kids needing you to them pushing you away, thus becoming more independent.

Use When:

- *Kids are afraid of being alone*
- *They are dependent on you/others being with them*
- *They are in constant need of knowing where you are*

Why the Tool Works:

1. *The anxious mind gets into patterns.*

   Kids are creatures of habit. Once they get used to something, it's hard to get them to change. If they start needing you to be with them when they go upstairs, pretty soon they'll insist you do it every time, just because they are used to having it that way. The same goes for kids wanting to sleep in their parents' bed. It starts out as a fear of monsters, and eventually sleeping with parents becomes a habit that is very hard for kids to break. When you use tools like Over Checking, the pattern changes because your response to your child's anxiety changes. Instead of waiting for your child to come to you with his anxiety, you go to him. Instead of him asking you for help, you beat him to it by offering to help. This changes up the dynamic around your child's anxiety and allows new changes in behavior to develop.

2. *Kids are constantly striving toward independence.*

    This is a good thing. The fact that kids are biologically programmed for independence makes a big difference to an anxious child. Kids are meant to push you away. They are meant to take off the training wheels of life and wobble on their own. When it comes to anxiety, this is also true. Kids need to figure out how to handle fears on their own. They need to find a way to go upstairs alone. They need to learn how to fall asleep alone and how to fall back asleep once they've had a bad dream. Anxious kids not only need to do this, but deep down, they want to do this. Becoming independent is the goal of childhood, and when kids feel able to tackle things on their own, their self-esteem skyrockets. Kids will often say they don't want to do things alone, but that is just because they don't think they can. Once they experience the feeling of success, they will want to do more things on their own, because it makes them feel so much better.

3. *Reverse psychology works.*

    Reverse psychology is when you tell your child the opposite of what you want him to do. For example, if you want your child to eat his peas, instead of saying, "Eat your peas," you say, "I bet you can't eat three peas." This is often enough to make a child eat his peas just to prove you wrong. If implemented correctly, reverse psychology makes kids do all kinds of things you never thought they would do. Just as I mentioned in the previous section, kids are striving for independence; therefore, pushing against you feels natural to them. When they push against you and are able to succeed, they feel a surge of independence and want to try it again. Kids, especially stubborn kids, will love this tool, because you are essentially encouraging them to go against you. While this is not always an effective tool for brushing teeth (although it has been tried), it works great with anxiety. Reverse psychology is effective because you change up the dynamic around your child's anxiety. Instead of waiting for your child to come to you with anxiety, you go to them. When this happens, you throw off their pattern of needing you and allow them to become independent.

How to Implement:

Step 1: Choose one thing your child is afraid of.

Focus on one area of your child's anxiety at a time. For instance, if your child is afraid of going upstairs alone and is also afraid of falling asleep in his own bed, decide which anxiety seems stronger or the most difficult to parent. If he makes you or a sibling go with him every time he goes upstairs and that is more disruptive, choose that fear and focus on the sleeping later. However, if your child's fear of going upstairs is extremely intense and you think the tool might overwhelm him, start with something simpler. Choosing a simple task provides momentum on which a child can build. If sleeping in his own bed is not one of his more severe areas of anxiety, you can start there, and it's quite possible the other things will become easier as well. Success breeds success when it comes to anxiety.

Step 2: Change the dynamic.

This is where the reverse psychology comes in. If your child is in a pattern of saying, "Mommy, will you go upstairs with me?" switch it up by saying, "Sam, please don't go upstairs without me. I need to go with you." You have to catch Sam before he asks you, but when you tell him not to go upstairs alone, he will give you a strange look, like you've got three heads. Sam is used to you pushing him away, but now you are clinging to him, and kids aren't fond of clinging. You are asking him to wait for you to do something (which kids also despise), and suddenly Sam is in a strange position. Should he wait for you to go with him, or should he push you away? By saying, "No you don't. I can go alone," he is pushing you away while also becoming more independent. If he says he can go alone, argue with him. Say, "No, Sam, don't do it! Wait for me." This only urges him on. Now your child is invested in going upstairs alone, when you couldn't have begged him to do it before.

Step 3: Invest in the process until the fear has been surpassed.

The hardest part of this process is being willing to go upstairs with your child if he wants you to. When you say, "No, Sam. Don't go upstairs alone," and he says, "Okay. Come with me," you have to be willing to do it. But as you do it, make sure to keep the dynamic the same. As you are walking upstairs, say, "I'm so glad you wanted me to come with you. I really don't think you should come up here alone." If you notice your child becoming more afraid of going upstairs alone, try lightening things up. If you are too serious with this tool, it may make your child more anxious. Instead, use humor and playfulness with your child. Also, if you are frustrated and grudg-ingly go upstairs the same way you have in the past, the tool will be ineffective. Even if your child wants you to go upstairs with him, when he takes one step away from you, say, "Please come back, Sam. Really. You're scaring me." This strengthens the tool even more, because kids love to scare their parents. Chances are he'll take several more steps away from you, all the while doing the very thing he was afraid to do before.

What You Will Find:

Changing the dynamic with anxious kids works beautifully. The anxiety process is centered around kids coming to parents and parents pushing kids away. When you switch it up by going to kids instead of them coming to you, they have no choice but to push you away. This tool also works beautifully around bedtime, when kids routinely call for their parents. Instead of waiting for them to call, go into their room every three minutes and say, "Are you okay? I was just check-ing." Pretty soon they'll say, "Get outta here. I'm trying to sleep!" While checking every three minutes takes a lot of effort on your part, it will be worth it in the end. Whenever you're stuck in a negative anxiety pattern with your child, changing the dynamic will lessen the intensity of the anxiety cycle. Giving anxious kids something different than what you've been giving them will allow something new to develop, and within that, independence is formed.

Tool #11:
Naming the Anxiety

Worry is a cycle of inefficient thoughts whirling around a center of fear.

—*Corrie Ten Boom*

Naming the Anxiety gives anxiety a name so kids can gain objectivity. A name such as "Worry Walter" helps kids see that anxiety comes and goes instead of it being present all the time.

Use When:

- *Children are overcome with fear*
- *They feel like something is wrong with them*
- *They respond well to humor*

Why the Tool Works:

1. *Anxiety can be very confusing.*

   What is anxiety? It can't be seen. It can't really be measured, and all kids can tell you is how they feel. They tell you about a stomachache, a headache, or that they can't sleep at night. They tell you about their scary thoughts, and you watch them become fidgety and irritable because of them. Anxiety is a list of symptoms even adults have a hard time understanding. Therefore, giving anxiety a name helps children understand it better. They can put a label on it and see that it comes and goes instead of getting all tangled up in it.

2. *Naming anxiety brings it down to a child's level.*

   When you use words like worry or fear instead of anxiety, you begin bringing anxiety down to a child's level. You can further bring anxiety down to a child's level by giving it a child-friendly name that makes it easier to understand. Names such as "Worry Walter" or "Scaredy Sally" help kids develop a mental image of what they are experiencing. They can put a face to their worry and begin seeing it more clearly. A mental image also takes the power out of the worry, as they can see that "Worry Walter" just shows up sometimes and makes them feel jumpy and nervous but that he leaves again, making them feeling calm. Seeing that "Worry Walter" comes and goes helps kids understand there's nothing "wrong" with them. They just have a "Worry Walter" that sometimes shows up but is often not there.

3. *Humor works wonders.*

   Humor and anxiety can't coexist. They are on opposite ends of the spectrum so when you add humor, anxiety will lessen. Humor breaks the cycle of anxiety and gives a huge amount of relief to anxious kids. If they can learn to laugh at themselves, they are much more likely to move through anxiety rather than let it debilitate them. One girl I work with said, "There I go again, worrying about what my new teacher is going to be like." She had a pattern of worrying every year before school started, and since she was aware of this, she was able not to let it overtake her. Instead, she made light of it by saying, "Worry Wanda loves to pop up at the beginning of school. She will go away in a few days." If a child can gain this type of insight, his anxiety might still show up, but it will be much less powerful.

How to Implement:

Step 1: Find a name for your child's anxiety.

This is the best part of the tool because you and your child can have fun with it. When your child is calm and in a light mood, talk about possible names for his anxiety. Say, "Let's give your worry a name." Offer suggestions of funny names or the nemeses of their favorite superheroes as examples, but make sure your child is the one who comes up with the actual name. When you agree on a name, practice using the name whenever your child is feeling anxious. Say, "Patrick, is that you, or is that 'Bobblehead' talking?" This will help your child gain perspective on his anxiety. Or better yet, when your child is anxious, he will be able to point out that "Bobblehead" has shown up. "I think 'Bobblehead' is here," he might say to let you know he is feeling anxious. This ability to recognize his own anxiety will help him gain valuable insight.

Step 2: Help your child gain control of his anxiety.

It may be enough for your child to give his anxiety a name. That alone may allow him to feel less anxious and be able to gain some perspective. However, if your child's anxiety returns, you may need to help him gain control of it. If "Worry Walter" comes out and your child becomes overwhelmed with fear, develop a plan to tackle "Worry Walter." You can make "Worry Walter" out of clay and smash him, you can draw him and rip him up, you can stomp on the ground, yelling, "Worry Walter, go away!" This allows your child to gain power over his anxiety in a concrete way. Because anxiety is abstract, making it into something concrete helps kids understand it better. The other tools listed in this section can also be helpful.

Square Breathing (Tool #1) will help your child deal with "Worry Walter." So will Changing the Channel (Tool #3) and Brain Plate (Tool #12).

Step 3: Normalize your child's anxiety.

Anxiety can make kids feel very alone. They feel like they are the only one who feels this way and that other kids have it much easier. As a parent, you can help your child feel less alone by normalizing his anxiety. If you struggle with anxiety yourself, you can tell your child you also worry and can come up with a name for your own anxiety. The name can be similar to your child's (i.e., "Worry Walter" and "Worry Wanda"), and you can share your own experiences of when your anxiety shows up. For example, you can say, "Right before I had to do that presentation at work, 'Worry Wanda' showed up." You can take this a step further by saying, "So I did Square Breathing and felt much better." This both normalizes your child's anxiety and models how to handle it. Your child will see that you also struggle with fear but that you are willing to use tools to manage it.

What You Will Find:

Anxiety is dark, heavy, and overwhelming. If you can make it lighter and more manageable, it will go away much quicker. Giving anxiety a name helps kids not take their fear as seriously. When you take every emotion seriously, you will find the lighter emotions are easily clouded by the heavier ones. That's why making light of anxiety by giving it a name takes the power away from it. After all, having anxious feelings doesn't mean anything. For nonanxious people, anxiety can clue you in that something is wrong, but if that is the case for anxious people, something is always wrong. That's why giving it a name will help kids have fun, gain perspective, and calm down in the meantime.

Tool #12:
Brain Plate

No one ever sank under the burden of the day. It is when tomorrow's burden is added to the burden of today that the weight is more than one can bear.

—*George MacDonald*

Brain Plate is a way to organize what kids think about so they worry about only one day at a time. Kids divide their day into sections, such as: school, home, friends, and activities. They list what they need to focus on each day so they won't worry about things days, weeks, even months ahead.

Use When:

- *Children are overwhelmed with future events*
- *They can't enjoy today because of the fear of tomorrow*
- *They have trouble staying in the present moment*

Why the Tool Works:

1. *The mind is meant to deal only with today.*

   For millions of years, humans had to be on constant alert for their survival. Dating back to the days of the caveman, if you went out of your cave in the middle of the night, you were in imminent danger. You might get struck over the head by another human or attacked by an animal, thus humans were in a constant state of hypervigilance. Fast forward several million years, and today's humans behave in similar ways. We live in constant fear that someone will break into our house (even though we have dogs and alarms) and that we'll get cancer (even though we just had a check-up) and so on. Basically, our situations have completely changed, yet our brains haven't. We are existing in today's society with an ancient brain, and this is especially hard on kids. Anxious kids constantly feel as if something bad is going to happen, and since they are not in immediate danger, they focus on future events as their source of danger.

2. *Future worries override the present moment.*

There are rarely any "problems" in the present moment. In the present moment, kids are playing with friends, they are brushing their teeth, taking a bath, or eating a Popsicle. Because the bath water is warm, there is running water to brush their teeth with, and there are friends around, anxious kids don't have to worry about much. But their minds convince them that the future might not be so great. On that field trip, the bus might break down, or on Friday's spelling test, they just might forget the answer. They don't know what is going to happen, so their mind begins spinning scenarios that totally take them out of the present moment.

3. *Learning to focus on today helps relax the mind.*

In order to manage anxiety, kids have to learn how to set boundaries for themselves. That's why this tool is so important. It helps kids set boundaries around their worries in a concrete way. Instead of having to wonder if they should be worrying about something, the tool makes the decision for them. It helps bring them back into the present moment and realize they will have a chance to worry about that thing, just not today. Knowing there is a time and place to worry helps kids let go of worrying about something all of the time. Having a specified day/time in which to worry will help anxious kids stay in the moment. One child said, "I worry about my spelling test only on Thursday nights now," after I taught him the Brain Plate technique. He knew when he was going to allow himself to worry, and knowing that he had that time allowed him to enjoy his week.

How to Implement:

Step 1: Help your child understand what happens when the mind is overloaded.

The simplest way to teach kids this tool is to help them understand that their brain is much like a dinner plate. I like to explain it to kids like this: "If I sat a plate in front of you and put a week's worth of food on it, what would that look like?" Kids love to draw this out, adding waffles, cereal, ice cream, and pot roast all piled up on the same plate. At some point kids usually say, "Gross!" because it is gross, but that is the same thing we do to our minds. Then I say, "Now if I made you eat that entire plate of food, what would happen?" Kids will say, "I'd get sick," and to that I say, "Exactly. But you know what? That's what you are doing to your mind. You are making your mind worry about a week's worth of worries, and your mind is feeling yucky because of it." That is why kids stress. That's why their stomachs hurt, their heads hurt, and they can't sleep. They have overloaded their minds with more than they can handle. You can explain Brain Plate just like I did above or choose your own way. The point is to help your child understand what an overloaded mind looks like and how he is doing the same thing to himself.

Step 2: Make a Brain Plate for your child.

I like to use paper plates for this because they are easy to write on, and I like the fact that they are actual plates. Divide the plate into four sections: *Home, School, Friends, Family,* and draw lines in between the sections with a pen or marker. The sections may be different, for example, if your child goes to dance lessons every day and it is a source of worry. The section headers are not as important as formulating the different parts of your child's life. Then (in pencil) begin to fill in what is on your child's plate for TODAY. If he has a math test today, write that in the school section. If he has a play date today, write that in the friend section. If he is watching a movie with the family, write that in the family section, etc. Once you have filled out the sections, encourage your child to think only about those things today. The only reason he would need to think about something tomorrow would be if he needs to do something for it today. For example, he may need to study for a test tomorrow or may need to practice the violin for tomorrow's recital. Otherwise, those events should not be on today's plate.

Step 3: Refer back to Brain Plate when your child is experiencing stress.

The reason your child used a pencil to fill out his plate was so you could fill out the plate on a daily basis. Especially when you first start using the tool, it's a good idea to fill out the plate regularly. This helps your child get into the hang of filling out the plate and of learning to think only about things that pertain to today. You can either sit down with your child on a daily basis or have your child do the activity independently. When I work with teenagers, I use this tool to help them with the stress of academics in addition to all of the social pressures of high school. Brain Plate has been a huge help for them. Just as Square Breathing can be used throughout a lifetime, so can Brain Plate. Even if your child has gotten out of the habit of doing the activity each day, you can always pull it back out when you need to. When your child is worrying about the future, remind him of Brain Plate and even model using it yourself.

What You Will Find:

If you don't set boundaries around worries, they will consume an anxious child. Future events will be all they think about, and they will miss out on a plethora of positive experiences as a result. Just like in the tool Worry Time, when you designate a specific time for worrying, kids will relax. They know they will be able to deal with their fears at a certain time, just not now. Knowing they can deal with Friday's worry on Friday, they won't lose the rest of the week worrying about it. You can help them with this by saying, "When do we think about Friday's worries?" When your child says, "Friday!" you will know you have gotten the tool across.

Tool #13:
Run Fast! Jump High!

Movement is a medicine for creating change in a person's physical, emotional, and mental states.

—*Carol Welch*

Run Fast! Jump High! is a way to implement exercise into the daily routine so anxious kids have a way to release their excess mental and physical energy.

Use When:

- *Children have excess energy*
- *They are facing an anxiety-producing event*
- *They are "keyed up" much of the time*

Why the Tool Works:

1. *Anxiety is energy.*

   Anxious kids have lots of energy. They talk incessantly, spin with excitement, and blow up with frustration. What comes out of anxious kids is intense and, without physical outlets, they end up spinning out of control. A symptom of anxiety is being "keyed up," and the average child will become even more "keyed up" before an anxiety-producing event. Kids who don't do well with change will start surging with energy weeks before school lets out and weeks before it starts back up again. Their birthday party and the holiday season will cause them to surge even more. When this surge of energy isn't released, it can come out in disastrous ways. Anxious kids will have meltdowns, wreak havoc on morning routines, and will bait parents into arguments simply because they are spinning with energy. By allowing your child to release his energy before it surges, your child will be much calmer, and his reactions will be less intense. When energy is released, anxiety decreases.

2. *A tired mind is a happy mind.*

When kids have spinning minds, they are irritable, easily frustrated, and reactive. When their minds relax, anxious kids are happier, more amenable, and less reactive. That's because when anxious kids are tired (or sick), they don't have the energy to fight all the battles they are used to fighting. They let things go, don't feed off every little thing, and are more accepting of the actions of others. Their energy is depleted, and having less energy helps anxious kids feel and act much better. Therefore, keeping anxious kids active is a recipe for a happier child. Unless it's 106 degrees outside or your child has a physical ailment, putting kids in situations where their energy can be drained (such as all-day summer camps) will result in better moods and less time for worry.

3. *Exercise releases endorphins.*

Any pediatrician will tell you that physical activity is crucial to a child's physical development. What they won't tell you is that physical activity is just as crucial to a child's emotional development. Physical activity releases endorphins, and endorphins are the key to helping anxious kids feel better. Endorphins are neurotransmitters produced in the brain that reduce pain. Pain can be either physical or psychological; regardless, endorphins will reduce it. Even when exercise occurs only for a short period of time, overall moods are improved as a result. When exercise lasts over thirty minutes, the highest benefits of endorphins will be seen. Endorphins are the reason many anxious adults run, do triathlons, and hike mountains. Even though they may not be in the mood for a 6:00 a.m. run, they get up anyway, knowing their body and mind will feel better as a result. This is the same for anxious kids. They may not want to go to the soccer game, but they'll feel much better after they do. They may not want to do 8:00 a.m. swim team, but they'll have a better day if they do.

How to Implement:

Step 1: Find an activity your child enjoys.

Some kids love sports. Other kids, not so much. If your child is the sports type, you are in luck. Sign him up for any sport he wants to play, and allow him to indulge in the benefits of a physical and emotional release. If your child is not the sports type, you'll have more of a challenge. Dance classes, karate, tae kwon do, and swim team are all great outlets for kids who aren't into team sports. Jumping on a trampoline, walking, riding a bike, skateboarding, and going to the park are also great options. The key is to find something your child likes and let him invest in the activity. Buy him a new skateboard or assign him the job of walking the dog every afternoon to earn extra allowance. Once a child invests, he will more likely want to do the activity.

Step 2: Make physical exercise part of your routine.

If you have an anxious child, your routine should include physical activity. It's not enough for your child to go to school, come home, do homework, and then play Legos or computer games. Even if it's taking a walk around the block, anxious kids need to be physically active, especially at the end of their school day. The stress of the school work itself, plus who played with whom at recess, what someone said at lunch, what happened in the pick-up line; those thoughts need to get burned off after school so they don't brew inside your anxious child's mind for the rest of the evening. If your child is resistant, exercise with him. By exercising with him, you are modeling both physical and emotional health. You can even say, "When I'm doing something active, I am in a better mood," to help your child understand the benefits. If your child wakes up with high levels of energy, implement a morning exercise routine to help burn off some of the energy. This is especially helpful for kids who have a hard time sitting still in class. Their morning routine can include doing one hundred jumping jacks, running around the yard five times, or riding their bike to school. The point being that burning off energy as it comes is better than waiting for it to build up, then trying to get rid of it all at once.

Step 3: Make it fun.

There's nothing worse than being forced to do something, and kids are forced to do things all day long. They have to do class work, listen to the teacher, and use the restroom only when it doesn't disturb the class. Having to do required things after school is not only frustrating for kids, it's also hard for parents to enforce. This is why it's so important to make exercise fun, and if implemented right, kids won't even realize they're doing it. After all, playing is exercise, and kids love to play. Playing a game of tag in the yard or a game of "Shark" in the pool is exercise. Exercise can also include stopping by the park on the way home from school or riding a bike to a friend's house. The goal of exercising for an anxious child is to 1) release excess energy, and 2) release endorphins. If your child is able to do both of those things, mission accomplished.

What You Will Find:

By implementing an exercise routine, you help reduce your child's anxiety surge significantly. Instead of allowing energy to build up, you allow energy to be released on a daily basis. You can also help your child become more rational during an anxious moment by saying, "Run the length of the yard five times and back, then we'll talk about your worry." This helps burn off your child's extra energy so he's able to talk more rationally about his fears. This is an especially useful tool for Outward Processors who are in constant need of an immediate release. By delaying their outward processing, you allow them to release their excess anxiety on their own instead of needing you to help them. Eventually, anxious kids will recognize their need for physical activity on their own. Kids will say, "I'm feeling jumpy. I'm going to run around the yard for a minute." This allows them to notice their own need for an energy release and be able to monitor themselves more closely.

Tool #14:
The Worry Expert

Worry is an addiction that interferes with compassion.

—*Deng Ming-Dao*

The Worry Expert is a way for kids to gain objectivity on their anxiety by helping someone else solve a similar problem. By offering suggestions to other kids, anxious kids can learn what will work best for them in a given situation.

Use When:

- *Children are consumed with their own anxiety*
- *They aren't using your suggestions*
- *They enjoy being a leader*

Why the Tool Works:

1. *The anxious mind is not objective.*

   Anxious kids aren't sure how to feel better. If they are afraid of sleeping in their own bed, instead of trying to figure out why they are scared, they would just as soon jump in bed with you. When they are anxious, kids simply try to get out of anxious situations rather than think of ways to resolve their anxiety. Even when you try to help them come up with solutions, they often say, "I don't know," or "Nothing works." This leaves parents frustrated, because their anxious kids don't seem motivated to help themselves. Part of this is because the anxious mind is not objective. The other part is that kids would rather jump in bed with you than sleep in their own bed, so they are often not really motivated for things to get better. This all changes when you ask an anxious child to help another child with his anxiety. Kids love to be experts, even for just a few moments, so giving them a chance to do just that will make great things happen.

2. *Helping others makes kids feel good.*

When I was an elementary school teacher, I knew the easiest way to make a child feel good was to ask him to do something. Whether it is running a note to the office or organizing textbooks, anxious kids love to help. This all changes in middle school, but while kids are young, helping others is one of their favorite things to do. This dynamic is the same when anxious kids help other kids with their anxiety. As I've said before, one of the most effective things I can do as a therapist is share stories about the struggles other anxious kids are having. Suddenly, the debilitated kid in front of me has all the answers! He knows just what will work for the other kid and becomes so interested in the other kid getting better, he starts trying things on his own. "I took a flashlight with me to bed last night," he'll say. "Did the other kid try that?" Mind you, I have spent several sessions trying to encourage this child to sleep in his own bed, but he adamantly refused because of the "monsters" underneath it.

3. *By learning to help others, anxious kids help themselves.*

It is so much easier to see the solutions to problems if the problems aren't yours. You know what your friend should do about her marriage or what she should do about parenting her child.

It's not that you are a "know-it-all"; it's that things are so much clearer when you are not in the midst of them yourself. This goes the same for kids. Kids can easily see how another child might feel better about a problem. They know monsters aren't real, and if they could only convince the other kid of that, they know he would feel better. Therefore, when they help another child with his problems, they are essentially helping themselves. If they can convince a child there's nothing to worry about, they will begin to believe it too. They will start seeing solutions to their own anxiety, since they were able to see solutions for the other child.

How to Implement:

Step 1: Tell your child about another anxious child.

If you happen to be a good storyteller, you are really going to like this tool. Kids love stories and learn better through hearing stories than they do much else. Stories allow kids to learn about other kids, thus learning about themselves. Therefore, if you are a good story-teller, you can help your child learn about his anxiety through stories you tell about yourself or other kids you have known. These stories are different from the other stories you tell your child in that they serve a purpose…but you don't want your child to know that. If you say, "You really seem to be struggling with anxiety, so I'm going to tell you a story that might help you gain some perspective," you lose the story's effect. Instead say, "You wouldn't believe who worried when he was a kid." This entry point creates lots of interest for kids. "Who? Who?" is what most kids will ask, and once you have their attention, you are ready to begin your story. If you are not the best storyteller, find an age-appropriate book about a child who worries (there are plenty out there) and read it to your child. If your child feels forced in any way to listen or read, the tool will not be as effective as if you planted a seed and they became interested on their own.

Step 2: Ask your child for suggestions.

Some parents do such a great job telling the story they don't even need to ask for suggestions. Their kids blurt out, "Why didn't you just take a flashlight into the forest?" or "Why doesn't she just take her dog upstairs with her?" in reaction to the story being told. If this doesn't happen for your child, say, "This kid is so scared. What do you think would help him?" Kids will usually fall right in and tell you what the other kid is doing wrong and how he could get over his fear in a flash. Ideally, you will tell a story of a child with the same issue your child is facing. If your child is more defensive, you may have to start with something a little off-topic to get your child invested. For example, children with Relational Anxiety are often guarded about their anxiety; therefore, I begin with telling them about friendship issues when their anxiety is really about getting love and affection from parents. Then, once they are more comfortable, I slant the story to be more closely related to their fears.

Step 3: Allow your child to help the other child, thus helping himself.

If there is a real-life situation where your child can be of help, you will be able to see immediate results. If his younger sister is having trouble being away from you, you may not even have to tell a story. Your anxious child can help her in real time. Kids love to help, especially when they know something the other child does not. When I teach anxious kids Square Breathing, they will often go home and teach their younger sibling to use it when having a meltdown. Parents will say, "He's taught our whole house how to Square Breathe," and when he comes back in my office, he can't wait to tell me too. "My sister has a lot of anger," he might say, "so I taught her how to do Square Breathing." If I've told him about another kid I'm working with who's also angry, he'll ask, "Did you teach him Square Breathing?" as a means to help. If you tell a story, have your child invest in his suggestions by rewriting the way the story ends or allowing your child to verbally express what would happen if the character in the story followed his advice.

What You Will Find:

Stories do wonders for kids. So does the opportunity to help others. Anxious kids feel alone in their fears, and when you normalize their anxiety, they feel less alone and are able to connect not only to other kids, but also more closely to themselves. The majority of kids don't realize there are tons of anxious kids out there who are struggling with the same issues they are. When they realize this, they get a sense of relief and begin to see that nothing is "wrong" with them. They will see that they are okay just as they are and that things will get better for them in the very near future.

Tool #15:
Feelings Check-In

Knowledge is being aware that fire can burn; wisdom is remembering the blister.
—*Leo Nikolaevich Tolstoy*

Feelings Check-In is a set time everyday where both you and your child choose three feelings to discuss. This tool raises emotional intelligence, as well as the connection with your child.

Use When:

- *Children lack emotional awareness*
- *They avoid talking about their feelings*
- *They enjoy one-on-one time with parents*

Why the Tool Works:

1. *Emotional awareness can be taught.*
   Some kids aren't good at talking about their feelings. When you ask them how they feel, they say, "I don't know." If you ask them why they hit their sister, they say, "She hit me first!" I was working with an eight-year-old boy recently who had a habit of saying "I don't know" every time I asked a question. After his third or fourth "I don't know," I said, "What if you did know?" He thought for a second and said, "I guess I was scared." We then were able to begin a conversation about why the situation was scary and what he could have done to help himself feel

better. If I had just let him stick with the "I don't know," we wouldn't have gotten to his feeling and never would have been able to address the issue. Many kids say "I don't know" because they really don't know why they are afraid, frustrated, sad, etc. Other kids just don't want to talk about it. Regardless, you can help kids learn to identify their feelings and express them in appropriate ways.

2. *Talking about feelings helps kids understand themselves.*

Saying things out loud can be extremely helpful. It's not just because the person listening can understand us better, it's because saying things out loud helps us understand ourselves better. This goes the same for kids. Anxious thoughts are swirling in their minds, and when they are able to express them verbally, they gain perspective. Identifying how they feel and being able to voice it helps kids figure out their own problems. "That makes sense," one child said to me recently. "I got scared at the last sleepover. No wonder I have been feeling nervous this week." This kind of awareness is extremely valuable in that the more kids know and understand themselves, the more they will be able to manage their own anxiety.

3. *Modeling emotions helps kids learn it's okay to talk about their feelings.*

The fact that parents have to eat, sleep, and have emotions is shocking to kids. Nonetheless, this is important for kids to understand. The fact that you get angry, frustrated, and irritated is important for your child to know. The fact that you handle those emotions appropriately is even more important for your child to recognize. The fact that you get angry when someone cuts you off in traffic or worried before you have to give a presentation at work, yet you handle those emotions appropriately, teaches kids how to handle their own emotions appropriately.

How to Implement:

Step 1: Buy or make feelings cards.

Kids, especially ones who aren't good at expressing their emotions, are going to need some help identifying how they feel. If you simply ask, "How was your day?" you're likely going to get "Fine" as a response. Furthermore, if you ask how kids feel, they will generally say "Fine" as well. Several years ago I heard that "fine" means **F**eelings **I**n **N**eed of **E**xpression, and for kids, this is largely true. But to expect kids to automatically know how to identify their feelings is often too much to ask. Instead, an effective way to help kids identify and express their feelings is to give them concrete choices to choose from. In my office, I have a set of feelings cards called "Feeleez" (www.feeleez.com) that includes twenty-five feelings faces kids can choose from. There are other types of feelings cards online, or you can make your own. If you choose to make your own though, include the face with the name of the feeling. The face helps kids understand how feelings are expressed and helps them better identify other people's feelings as well.

Step 2: You choose three feelings, they choose three feelings.

This step is a great way to connect with your child. You can either choose your feelings first or allow your child to. Regardless, it's important to choose your feelings too, as it is a great way to model emotional intelligence. In choosing them, I would encourage you to choose at least one negative feeling such as worried, angry, frustrated, embarrassed, overwhelmed, etc., along with one positive feeling, such as excited, happy, calm, etc. The other feeling can be anything else you choose. Choosing at least one negative and one positive feeling allows kids to see that both negative and positive feelings can exist within the same day. After you choose your three, go through each one and say why you felt that way. For example say, "I felt worried when I thought I was going to be late for work" or "I felt sad when I saw a lost dog on the side of the road." Then have your child take their turn and do the same thing.

Step 3: Begin identifying feelings outside of the check-in time.

It is a great step when a child says, "I don't need the feelings cards. I already know how I feel." Especially when he is able to choose words such as embarrassed, overwhelmed, or jealous without needing prompting. A nine-year-old girl who had a difficult time expressing her emotions came in from school after only a week of doing *Feelings Check-In* saying, "I know my three feelings for the day. Can we go ahead and do our check-in?" A comment like that lets you know your child is becoming more emotionally intelligent. She was becoming aware of her feelings throughout the day and was wanting to share it with her parent, something she was not able to do before.

What You Will Find:

Once kids are able to share how they feel, they not only understand themselves better, but you also understand them better. If your child can tell you he's jealous of his sister, you will be much more understanding than if he just hits his sister and walks away. From saying he's jealous, you can talk about ways to help him feel more secure in his relationship with his sister by saying things like, "When do you feel the most jealous of her?" and "What would make you feel more loved and appreciated?" Being able to identify and express emotions is one of the most important steps in helping an anxious child, and this tool provides an important step in helping your child do just that.

Conclusion

. . . .

"I used to be so overwhelmed when Samantha talked about her worries. I felt the need to answer all of her questions, but now I use The Five Question Rule to set boundaries and even do Square Breathing myself! At first I thought the tools would just benefit her. Now I realize how much they've benefitted me."

"It took a while to understand that my son's anxiety goes in cycles. I would get so worked up when he started worrying, but now I know if I just use the tools, he'll ride it out and feel okay again. I felt like I was playing into his anxiety for so long. Now that I know what to do about it, I am able to be strong for him."

When kids are in the midst of anxiety, it's hard to believe things will get better. It's hard to believe your child will smile again and that the huge fear that has debilitated him will finally be overcome. But things do, in fact, get better for anxious kids. Given the proper support and tools, anxious kids can go from debilitated to confident, from scared to calm. There will be bumps in the road, no doubt, but once you have the tools in place, the bumps will be less disruptive, and your child will seem less thrown off track.

When nine-year-old Sarah first came to see me, she was terrified by fears that were beyond her years. She worried about death, going to college, getting a job, and how she would afford a house. She was so worried about the future that she'd written out a goal sheet that included her five-year, ten-year, even her twenty-year goal of becoming a doctor. She talked about her fears continually, and by the time her parents made an appointment, they were overwhelmed and didn't know what to do. "She's obsessed with the future," her dad reported. "We've tried everything, from reasoning with her to refusing to talk about it. Nothing seems to work."

In my first session with Sarah, I saw how worked up she became in talking about the future. She brought in her goal sheet and carefully told me how she was going to take advanced classes in high school, go to Stanford for college, and become an orthopedic surgeon afterward. While she was talking, I noticed her shoulders tighten up and her breathing shorten. I listened carefully while she explained her goals, then showed her how to do *Square Breathing*. After doing three rounds of Square Breathing together, I saw Sarah's body relax and her breathing become slower. As I do with most kids, I encouraged Sarah to go home and teach her parents Square Breathing, and when she came back for the second session, I learned she'd not only taught her parents, but she'd also taught her sister. The whole family had been doing Square Breathing together every evening at bedtime.

Sarah came back for the second session with her goal sheet in hand, but after doing three rounds of Square Breathing together, she was able to talk about other things, such as how her school day went and what she was looking forward to over the weekend. I praised Sarah for talking about the immediate future and encouraged her to stay in the present and focused on each day by teaching her Brain Plate, which she took home and shared with her parents. By the time Sarah came back for the third session, she reported feeling much better. She was using the tools I had taught her and didn't feel the need to bring her goal sheet to our sessions anymore. Her mother, however, was still struggling with how to deal with Sarah's anxiety.

"She still asks repeated questions," her mother said. "I'm not sure if it is just a habit or if she is really worried." In talking more with Sarah's mother, I realized they had spent so much time talking about her fears that they didn't talk about much else. So I taught Sarah's mother The Five Question Rule along with Changing the Channel, and within a couple of weeks, Sarah was rarely talking about her anxiety at all. The tools had helped her mother set boundaries around her questions as well as change the direction of the conversation, which made a huge difference in the way they communicated. In fact, Sarah and her mother started talking about happy things for the first time in months.

Not all kids will make connections as fast as Sarah did. Not every parent will be able to implement the tools so effectively either. However, anxiety can and will get better if parents are willing to learn about their child's anxiety and use the right tools to help him manage it. Don't be surprised to see your child become a Worry Expert by encouraging members of the family to do Square Breathing or telling you to Change the Channel when you're stressed out about the traffic on the interstate. What you teach kids will stick, and when it comes to tools for reducing anxiety, that's a good thing.

The fact is, you will have a profound effect on your child's anxiety. Whether your child is struggling with daily bouts of anxiety or twice-a-year flare-ups, your child will be looking to you for help. If you are informed and equipped with the right tools, you will be able to give your child the support he needs. You will be able to help him ride out the rough times and learn to enjoy the good times. You will also be there to see your precocious, amazing child overcome his biggest fears. When he looks at you with a big smile and says, "See, I did it!" you will know your commitment to helping your child through those anxious times has made all the difference.

Checklist of Anxiety Symptoms

Children struggling with anxiety may exhibit the following:

☐ Pessimism and negative thinking patterns, such as imagining the worst, overexaggerating the negatives, rigidity and inflexibility, self-criticism, guilty thoughts, etc.

☐ Constant worry about things that might happen or have happened

☐ Physical complaints, such as stomachaches, headaches, fatigue, etc.

☐ Avoidance behaviors, such as avoiding things or places or refusing to do things or go places

☐ Sleeping difficulties, such as difficulty falling or staying asleep, nightmares, or night terror

☐ Irritability

☐ Perfectionism about simple tasks, including having to make letters and words perfectly, tearing up a drawing to redo it, having an event go exactly the way they want it to go

☐ Excessive clinginess and separation anxiety

☐ Poor memory and concentration

☐ Withdrawal from activities and family interactions

☐ Eating disturbances, such as a sudden refusal to eat certain foods or a change in eating patterns

Think Sheet

1. What did you do?_____
_____
_____

2. When you did that, what did you want?_____
_____
_____

3. List three other things you could have done:

     1._____
     _____

     2._____
     _____

     3._____
     _____

4. What will you do next time?_____
_____
_____

Acknowledgments

. . . .

This book was born in my own childhood, when fears were looming around every corner. It was nourished in grad school, when I learned why those fears existed and what I could do about them. It grew legs and walked when I first began working with worried kids and their parents. To the brave children who had the courage to open up about their fears and to the parents who tirelessly made efforts to help them, I owe this book to you.

I would also like to thank my wonderful agent, Liz Trupin-Pulli, who believed in a first-time author and, through her wisdom and effort, found my book the perfect home. I am also indebted to my editor, Shana Drehs, whose passion and excitement for this project made all the difference. Her ideas, suggestions, and enthusiasm guided me through long hours of editing and allowed me to see the light at the end of the tunnel. To all those at Sourcebooks, including Anna Klenke, thank you for making this dream a reality.

I am grateful for my dear colleagues, Daniel Barton and Bethany Ezell, who were there to continually listen and encourage me through the writing of this book. I could not have done it without you. To my longtime supervisor and mentor, Melinda Borthick, who helped a poor graduate student believe she could one day have a private practice. She led me to the Nashville Psychotherapy Institute, where I befriended the late Jill Baker, among other wonderful colleagues, and found a home in the Nashville community.

There are many others. Kristi Leikvoll, Terry Maroney, Sara Cohan, Sara Atherton, Kris Mumford, Yuki Mori, and many more who were there to offer support, treat me to coffee, and keep me sane through the writing of this book. To my dad, who taught me to dream big; my brother Shane, who never ceases to make me laugh; and my sister Natalie, who always keeps me in line. And lastly, I'd like to thank my mother, who stayed up late, listened without tiring, and was always there for her worried child. May every parent get it right—just as you did.

Index

About the Author

Allison Edwards is a licensed professional counselor and registered play
therapist with specialized training
in working with children, adolescents, and families. She received a
bachelor's degree in education from
Northwest Missouri State and a
master's degree in counseling from
Vanderbilt University. She is an

Photo credit: Mary Claire Crow

adjunct professor in the Human Development Counseling program
at Vanderbilt University, and she maintains a full-time private practice with children of all ages.